Also by Dennis Collins

The Unreal McCoy

Turn Left at September

The First Domino

NIGHTMARE

by Dennis Collins

For Shirley
Have fun at the beach
6-23-12

www.theunrealmcoy.com

This is a work of fiction. Names, characters, places, and incidents either are the product of the author's imagination or are used fictitiously. Any resemblance to actual persons, living or dead, business establishments, events, or locales is entirely coincidental.

ISBN 978-0-615-62870-7

Cover design by Joe Hinds of Pony Express Photo
Interior design by Susan Leonard of Rose Island Bookworks

Printed in the United States of America

Acknowledgements

Many thanks to my good friend Joe Hinds of Pony Express Photo for the cover design. And I can't give enough thanks to my sometimes ruthless editors Susan Leonard, John Hodgins, and Diana Collins. I'm pleased to say that this work survived the scrutiny of Caseville Police Chief Jamie Learman and Cheeseburger Festival chairman Steve Louwers.

Bits and pieces of historical lore were supplied by Robert Heck and promotional support provided by Dave Lemaster.

Last, but certainly not least, many thanks to my writers group, The Huron Area Writers Group (HAWG), who slapped me around whenever I began to drift too far from the core story.

NIGHTMARE

CHAPTER 1

"He's going to do something horrible. I just know he is." Bonnie Prescott sat across the desk from Michael.

A sign on the door read, *O'Conner Investigations: Michael O'Conner, Prop.* The man behind the desk was the sole full-time employee of the private detective firm.

A couple years shy of his fortieth birthday and a couple inches short of 6 feet, Michael had bulked up his slender frame over the last couple of years with three-day a week free weight workout at the gym down the block. The extra muscle added to his confidence as well as his image. He kept his sandy-colored hair in a short business cut and always wore a tie in the office. He would remind the casual observer of a young Kirk Douglas. Looking fit and professional was good for business.

"If you think he's dangerous, you should be talking to the police," answered Michael.

Bonnie was a striking woman of classic beauty, stylishly feathered long blonde hair, a slender athletic build, and electric blue eyes. She might have been on the north side of thirty-five but it was more her air of confidence than her appearance that would suggest that. Her wardrobe was strictly Saks, dignified and understated.

"I wish it were that simple but he hasn't done anything illegal so the police won't even listen to me. I have no idea what he's up to. I just know that, whatever it is, he's going to hurt people. It's like a premonition, a really strong feeling and it gets stronger every day. They say that twins are sometimes like that. It's a phenomenon known as 'thought concordance.' It's not at all unusual in twins." There was a tremor in her voice.

Michael did his best to look serious. "That's a pretty strong accusation without much to go on. He gives you a very unsettling feeling but you're not even sure why. Has he been in psychiatric care? Do you have anybody who could back up your opinion? I mean, what would you expect from me?"

Bonnie shrugged and her eyes began to spill tears. Michael saw her desperation, offered a tissue.

"Why don't you take your time and tell me the whole story from beginning to end. What is it about your brother that troubles you so much?"

Bonnie Prescott let out a deep sigh and began.

"Ever since we were little kids I've known that Brian had problems dealing with people. I know him better than anyone in the world, we're twins, you know."

"I kinda guessed that," replied Michael.

He retrieved a legal pad from a desk drawer and fished a pencil out of the Michigan State coffee mug in front of him.

"I'm sure that he never even liked me. He wouldn't share his toys and he was always breaking my things on purpose. Mom took him to specialists to see if they could help but most of them said that he'd probably grow out of it. Brian spent a lot of his younger years in one kind of therapy or another. I remember overhearing my parents say it was some kind of chronic depression but the treatments ended before he entered high school and I don't think he ever got better. He just got better at hiding it.

He's never been arrested, or anything like that, but I'm sure he's done some terrible things. I remember he killed the neighbor's cat when he was ten, stoned it to death out in the alley. He was laughing the whole time. I saw him do it and he said that he'd kill me if I ever told on him. After watching that cat suffer I was scared out of my mind. I never said a word to anybody."

Bonnie stopped to take a drink of the bottled water that poked its neck out of her purse.

"Nobody ever got to know Brian. All through school he kept a low profile. He was a real loner. Few buddies, no girlfriends, didn't play sports, didn't even go to the senior prom. He was smart though and graduated near the top of his class. He was always so secretive. I think that the only one who knew how intelligent he was, was the principal.

After graduation I went on to an all-girl college in Detroit and he went out east to the Northeast Oceanic Institute in Maine. I tried to stay in touch but he seldom answered my letters. He majored in marine biology. It surprised me because he had never expressed an interest in that sort of thing. I actually still had some hope for him at that point. It sounded as if he'd found some direction in his life. Mom and Dad just sent him money and paid the bills. We only saw him a handful of times while he was away at school. He never came home during the summer, claimed he was an intern on some kind of oceanic survey. Our parents never questioned him. I think they were just glad that he wasn't home, causing trouble."

Michael rocked back in his chair. "So you really aren't sure what he was doing for those... what was it, four years?"

"Yes, it was four years and he really did spend all that time in school. I know that because he graduated with a Bachelor of Science degree. My parents and I attended his graduation. It was shortly before that when my grandmother died and we all inherited a lot of money."

Michael scribbled on the legal pad. "Was it enough money so you didn't have to work anymore?"

"Oh gosh yes. It was in the millions. Both Brian and I wound up with huge trust funds and our parents retired and became globe trotters. They went anywhere their passports would take them. As a matter of fact they were killed in a rock climbing accident in the Andes Mountains. The report said that their anchor point gave way and they were sharing a lifeline. They fell about 30 feet."

"I'm sorry to hear that."

Bonnie's eyes began to tear again. "Brian wasn't. It meant a bigger inheritance for him. The two of us became the sole heirs to everything. Brian's share included my grandparents' old fishery up north."

"Fishery?"

"My grandfather began as a simple fisherman right after the Second World War. Had a trawler and a little piece of water frontage with a dock on Wildfowl Bay up near Caseville. He was one of the first veterans to get into that business after the war and he just kept expanding. Built his home right there on the water and bought up any adjoining property he could get his hands on. Pretty soon he had about a dozen gill-netters wandering all over Saginaw Bay and Lake Huron hauling in fish by the tons. He supplied half the east coast with fresh lake perch and herring. But he didn't stop there; he bought a barge, put a big steam shovel-like thing on it and began a dredging business, making channels and putting in seawalls all up and down the shoreline. In the end he had something like over 300 acres with at least 1000 feet of frontage on the water."

"So your brother inherited a thriving fishing business."

"No. The fishery ceased doing business when the gill-nets were outlawed way back before we were born. I think it was sometime in the mid 1960s. My grandfather began buying up more property as more fisheries went out of business. And then the government stepped in and declared the entire area a Wetland and Migratory Fowl Refuge. They blocked any further sale of land to private parties and purchased any land that was for sale at a premium price so that nobody could build on it. Before long the whole area was completely overgrown with cattails and willows. My grandfather kept all of the land that he owned though, wouldn't sell it to the government. His dredging and seawall business was still growing. He installed lots of seawalls in years when the water was high and when the water was low, the dredging business went crazy. He did a lot if investing too. Whoever his advisor was, he was good because Grandpa kept getting richer and richer until the day he passed away. Never left the old house though. Neither did Grandma. She died there."

"And your brother still owns your grandparents' homestead?"

"Yes, it's grandfathered so the government can't do anything about it. That's where he's living now. It's the only private property in a 7 mile stretch. The highway's almost a half mile off of the bay at that point and so you can't even tell that there is a house back there."

Michael sighed. "Sounds pretty isolated."

"Very. There is a big electronic iron gate across the driveway now. Brian put that in a couple of years ago. I haven't been invited for a visit for a long time so I have no way of knowing exactly what is going on in there. The last time I saw the place Grandpa's trawler was still there along with his dredging equipment. I think he sold the other fishing boats but as far as I know all of that other stuff is still around."

"Why is it that you're so convinced that your brother is doing something illegal? Lots of water front homes have electronic gates"

Bonnie took another tug on the water bottle. "I just know him and know the way he does things. It was actually the gate across his driveway that sent up a flag for me. It's not out by the road where you can see it. It's hidden about 100 feet into the woods. People driving by on the highway don't even know it's there. He claims that he can't have it any farther from the house because there's a voltage drop if he has to run the power that distance, and it won't work. He's hiding something. Brian loves to hurt people for no other reason than to watch them suffer. He's obsessed with it. I think he's psychotic, pure and simple. And when Brian hides things, he has a sinister reason."

"You sound absolutely convinced but just suppose that there's nothing to it, like he may simply want to be left alone and nothing else. What if I spend all summer watching him and nothing unusual happens?"

"I still want to make sure that he's not hurting anybody.

I don't trust him. Don't worry, I'll pay you whatever your standard rate is for your time and expenses."

"That doesn't concern me, Miss Prescott. I'm actually hoping for your sake that there's nothing to discover. But before I agree to take your case I've got to be sure that I have the resources to properly investigate it, Can you give me a couple of days?

Bonnie answered immediately, "Can you let me know by the end of the week?"

"Absolutely. Oh. And one last question," said Michael, "Where were you guys raised? What city?'

"We all lived together in Detroit until Brian went away to college. When we were younger, us kids would spend a month or so at our grandparents' place every summer but it was just vacation. We never actually lived there."

CHAPTER 2

If one was to judge by the weather it seemed like late August, even the overhead power lines were sagging and dripping with humidity. But it was only the third week of July. The signs of a long hot summer were evident everywhere.

Brian Prescott wiped the sweat from his forehead. Things seemed to be going along pretty well. He had the old diesel engine muffled down enough so that the sound only carried a few hundred yards, even over the water. It was slow working alone and it would be a while before he could bring any hired hands on board. Before he could let anybody see what he was doing, he'd have to have a complete plan that included disposing of the bodies once he was done with his helpers. The indoor pen that he had built into the old boat house appeared to be holding up quite well. Three of the sides were already there when he moved in, sheet steel pilings driven all the way to bedrock.

Two months ago he had installed the reinforcement rod gate and the nine big fish had made it their comfortable home. He had just spent weeks constructing the giant floating artificial island that looked exactly like the endless miles of cattails growing in the shallows. The area that he was dredging covered about a half acre on the surface but it had to blend in seamlessly and be undetectable from the air.

The fly overs from the Department of the Interior weren't all that frequent but they did appear to be random and so he had to be ready at all times. The only thing predictable was that they only occurred on clear days and never before noon.

One more day and the dredging would be done. Then he could begin lining the area with the special cage that he would make from the old gill nets that were stacked to the ceilings of the storage sheds. That was the one job that he couldn't do alone. But with a good start and competent help, there would be no reason why the job couldn't be done in one day.

Brian had made a few stops at the local bars and kept his eyes open for a certain type of character. He'd recently befriended a couple of drifters who made their beer money by picking up odd jobs. Brian had them pegged as experienced construction workers whose frequent drinking habits made it difficult to keep a steady job or a steady girlfriend. These were the loner types who were generally paid under the table and were smart enough to keep quiet about who they were working for.

In the coming days Brian would feel these two out to see if they could be trusted and if he liked what he saw, he'd offer them the work. He'd need one or two helpers to finish his project and then they would have to die.

Back when Brian was just getting started on this project, he had tried to hire a man to help him do some work on the old diesel engine that powered the drag-link on his motorized dredging barge. The plan had been to get the work done and then kill the man so that there would be no witnesses to figure out Brian's plan. But it hadn't worked out according to the script. The mechanic had brought his boss along, a well-known and popular trucking firm owner, a guy who would immediately be missed if he disappeared. Brian didn't like the way that the transport owner seemed to be looking around and sizing up the place, he appeared far too interested in the layout. Brian had to come up with a story to keep the pair from seeing what he was up to so he told them that he had sold the old dredging rig "as is" to a salvage dealer and their services wouldn't be needed. When they asked if they could take a quick look anyway, Brian said that he didn't have time to show them around because he was late for an appointment. It was a close call.

The next week, Brian installed the electronic gate. His project was set back several weeks while he studied the diesel repair manuals and fixed the old engine himself. After almost a solid month of 15 hour days, 7 days a week Brian finally had things back on schedule.

Chapter 3

Michael O'Conner put in a call to Sergeant Albert McCoy at the First Precinct, Detroit Police Department.

The detective answered on the first ring. "Homicide – McCoy."

"Hey McCoy, this is Michael. I've got a real interesting case pending and I'm not sure about some of the logistic aspects. Can we get together later and chat for a bit?"

"Sure Mike. Me and Otis are planning on stopping at Eddie's Bar for a burger and beer after work. We'll be there around five if that works for you."

"Perfect. See you there." Michael always liked the ambience of Eddie's. It was a cop's bar and the food was good. The fact that Otis Springfield would be there was a big plus as well. Otis had recently been promoted to lieutenant but before that he and McCoy had been partners. Back in the old days they were known as the A-team.

Michael sat at his desk making notes about his conversation with Bonnie Prescott, adding observations about her demeanor and body language. He ran both Brian's and Bonnie's names through his background information resources as well as the names of their parents. There was nothing particularly ground-breaking in the results of his search but at least he had a snapshot of their lives. Bonnie had provided family photos taken after both her and

Brian's college graduations and Michael scanned them and included them in his file. They weren't very recent pictures but they were the most current likenesses of Brian available. Michael wrapped everything up in a professional-looking folder and headed out of his office at a quarter past four. The drive to Eddie's Bar usually took a little over a half hour so his timing was perfect.

The bar was just beginning to fill up with police officers, all in civilian clothes, from at least four different precincts. Michael grabbed a table on the opposite side of the room from the jukebox and ordered a pitcher of beer and three glasses. There was still a pretty good head on the pitcher when McCoy and Springfield came through the door. Smiling, they both headed in Michael's direction.

Otis Springfield was the first to speak. "You must have a serious problem if you've got a pitcher and frosted mugs waiting for us."

McCoy chimed in, "This will probably take more than just one pitcher. We don't work cheap, y'know."

For the next hour Michael described everything that went on during his interview with Bonnie Prescott including his observations of her state of anxiety and fear. He provided all the background that he was able to uncover on the family and then placed his hands on the table saying, "So what do I do next?"

"Actually you need to go back one more generation if you want to make any headway," said McCoy, "They're a Detroit family and people tend to get lost in a big city like Detroit. But the grandparents are small-town folks and more than that, they were prosperous small-town folks. Everybody in the area would have known their business and it's a safe bet that they all know that it's a grandson that inherited the place. He can keep to himself as much as he wants but it won't stop the local busybodies from knowing what he's up to."

"Or at least speculating," added Otis, "You said that this place is up by Wildfowl Bay, right? One of the local police chiefs up that way is a retired Detroit officer. I can get you connected with him and you can pick his brain. Those kind of guys love getting their teeth into a real puzzle from time to time. They miss the big city action even if they don't admit it."

"You might want to see what you can dig up from his college days too. It would give you a better picture of what his adult life is like." McCoy poured himself another beer. "The college itself won't be much help because of privacy policies but if you can get your hands on a yearbook, you can see who his classmates were and maybe contact some of them. You also mentioned some field experience that he supposedly had during his summer breaks. If he was on some sort of oceangoing research ship, you can interview the skipper and crew. There're lots of places that you can snoop around."

Michael made detailed notes on the tips that the two cops were feeding him. He began to feel a little more comfortable about taking on the case. At least he'd be able to get a reasonably accurate assessment of his subject.

McCoy offered, "That's one of the advantages you have as a private investigator over a police department. Without a crime, there's no way any regular police resources can become officially involved but all you need is a client. In almost every case these kinds of things lead to a dead end but if this woman is willing to cover the tab for a full-blown investigation, and if you think there could be something to it, I say go for it. Dig in and see what you can find. We can help out with some of our contacts and stuff and when I'm off duty I wouldn't mind sniffing around a little. It might be fun"

Otis stood up. "I'll send you a name or two in the morning. Give me until about ten or so to talk to my buddy and fill him in and then I'll forward the contact information. He's a good guy and a good friend. I'm sure you'll find him helpful."

CHAPTER 4

Brian had never actually killed anybody but he craved it so badly that he considered it a need. All his life he had kept a low enough profile to avoid any curiosity from the authorities and he knew the value of stealth. He took great pains to conceal the primeval yearnings that throbbed in his head and in his heart. As a young adult Brian became aware of these psychotic desires and fought to overcome or at least control them. His parents had raised him to respect human life and he certainly knew the difference between right and wrong. But his hunger was overwhelming, especially when the screaming in his head started. That always seemed to trigger his homicidal lust. He eventually learned to rationalize his thoughts of killing as long as his victim was a nobody, someone who the world would not miss.

Brian found Shorty in Bay City, a town about fifty miles south of his home. Shorty was a sometimes construction worker, a sometimes handyman, sometimes house painter, sometimes septic tank serviceman, but mostly a full-time bum. Shorty was known as the town drunk in at least a half dozen small towns. He hadn't had a driver's license in years. He simply couldn't stay sober long enough. An ugly little man at 5 feet 2 inches and about 110 pounds, Shorty was far from intimidating but that didn't stop him from constantly running his mouth and provoking people. It may have been only pity for his dwarfish size that saved him from getting pulverized in some alley. He drifted in and out of several communities. Sometimes he would vanish for months only to resurface and become a barstool fixture until his unemployment insurance ran out and sobriety forced him back into the ranks of the employed for a while. But it never lasted. Shorty would stay on a job long enough to collect a couple of paychecks and then it was a crap shoot as to whether he'd ever show up again. But Shorty was known as a hard worker and he worked cheap so there was always some kind of job available.

Brian didn't really have any use for a guy like Shorty but it was a good opportunity to test some of his plans and to see if the thrill justified the anticipation. It would be easy to snatch Shorty away with nobody noticing and he didn't seem to be the kind of guy that anybody would miss.

Bay City was big enough and far enough away from Brian's home that he could move around with anonymity but he still made it a point to keep just enough distance between Shorty and himself that nobody would connect them. The only time he actually talked to Shorty was when no one else was around. He was getting itchy to make his move but he had to make sure that he had all the angles covered.

Brian had just stepped away from the urinal, zipped up his pants and washed his hands in the men's room of Miller's Bar when Shorty came whistling through the door

"Hey, how's it goin'?" said the squeaky voice.

"Everything is great," responded Brian, drying his hands. "And you?"

"Gonna have to wrap it up early tonight. I dropped my last ten on a Keno ticket. Can you believe I got absolutely nothing? Got four bucks left."

Brian looked down at the little guy. "Would a twenty get you through the night?"

Shorty stepped back with a surprised look on his face. "Why would you loan me money? You don't know me. Only seen you around a few times. What's the catch?"

"The catch is that you keep quiet about it. I don't want everybody in the bar thinking I'm a soft touch. You seem like a guy that I could trust and it looked like you were having such a good time out there, I figure why stop now?"

Shorty reached out tentatively and gently plucked the twenty-dollar bill from Brian's outstretched hand. "Thanks, man."

Brian returned to the barroom and found a stool halfway down the bar from where Shorty was sitting. He nursed a bottle of Coor's Light and pretended to engross himself in the Tigers and Angels game on the television. Shorty went back to drinking beer and playing Keno, the electronic game that the state's Lottery Commission had installed in almost every bar. For a one-dollar wager you can win anywhere from one to one-million dollars and as long as your prize is under six-hundred dollars, you are entitled to an instant payout. His luck was up and down, losing some and winning here and there, just enough to keep his night going for another two hours.

Finally Brian decided to call it a night and stopped in the men's room on his way to the back door. He had just finished washing his hands again when Shorty popped through the door. "Hey man, I just hit a Keno ticket for seventy-two bucks. Here's your twenty back and thanks for the help."

Brian smiled, folded up the bill and stuffed it in his pocket. "You got a job?" he asked Shorty.

"Nah. Gonna start lookin' around tomorrow. You hear of anything out there?"

"Well, I'm looking for someone to help me get a couple of fishing boats ready. Nothing real complicated. Mostly just clean-up and painting and that sort of thing. Interested?"

Shorty looked at his shoes for a moment. "That's the kind of work I usually do but right now I don't have a way to get around. Are these boats right here in town? At one of the Marinas?"

"Nope, they're at my private dock. But if you can get away for a couple weeks there is a crew shack right on the dock that nobody's using right now. It's got complete living quarters, even cable television."

"Is it close to town? When I'm off work I like to stop by the local tavern from time to time, y'know."

"It's close enough and there's public transportation that runs right by the front door."

Shorty nodded his head a couple of times and asked. "What does it pay?"

"It starts at fifteen bucks an hour and if you're a good hand I just might hire you on as full-time maintenance. That would be a little more money. No promises though. I've got to see how this works out first."

The wheels turning in Shorty's head were almost visible. Fifteen dollars an hour was more than he'd ever made in his lifetime and an opportunity for a permanent job was something he hadn't considered possible anymore. He was seeing a chance to turn his life around. "I don't see how I can pass it up. When can I start?"

Brian replied, "I'm headed there right now. You can ride home with me and start first thing tomorrow. The living quarters are all set up and the refrigerator is full of beer. I even provide work uniforms. If you want the job, let's head for the parking lot."

Things were happening faster than Shorty could process them. He wasn't happy about being rushed like this but he was facing a decision about the best opportunity he'd seen in decades.

"I'll meet you out there as soon as I can grab my cigarettes and stuff off the bar."

"I'll be waiting out back. I'll be watching for you to come out the back door." Brian pulled the men's room door open and headed for the parking lot.

When Shorty went back to pick up his money he found the bartender standing there with the telephone in his hand yelling "Is there a Wallace Stueber in the bar?"

"That's me," hollered Shorty. He took the phone from the bartender. "Yeah. Hey, I just got a job. It's somewhere up north working on a fishing boat. It's big money, can't turn it down. I'm leaving right now, got a ride up there. I'll call as soon as I know more. Love ya. Bye."

"What took you so long?" asked Brian as Shorty climbed into the SUV passenger's seat.

"Ah, the bartender wanted to chitchat. I think he was fishing for a big tip because I just hit on a Keno ticket. Had a hell of a time getting away from him." Shorty never let anyone in on his personal life. He figured that things were less complicated if people thought he was all alone in the world. Keep it simple. He liked it that way.

The first stop that Brian made after leaving the bar was the corner party store to pick up a six-pack of Budweiser which he dropped in Shorty's lap when he returned to the car.

"This should keep you from getting dried out on the trip," he said with a smile.

Shorty nodded in appreciation.

Brian tried to get as much information out of Shorty as he could on the ride back to his place. Shorty told him that he had dropped out of a Detroit high school in the tenth grade and never bothered to finish and that was mainly what had kept him from getting a good job. He also said that his low blood pressure had kept him out of the military. At a young age, maybe nine or ten he had been taken out of his parents' home for reasons he never knew and had been raised in a series of foster homes until he was eighteen. He claimed that he had never been in trouble with the law except for some traffic tickets. He had spent several years working at a gas station owned by one of his foster parents' neighbors but the job ended when the old man retired and sold the business. Since then Shorty had never held a job for longer than six months.

When Brian asked if he'd ever been married or had any kids, Shorty's reply was, "I'm not cut out to be a family man."

Satisfied that Shorty was exactly the type of vagrant that he was looking for, Brian remained mostly silent for the remainder of the trip. He replayed the entire evening in his mind and was convinced that no one had seen him talk to Shorty in the bar and that he had kept a low-enough profile that nobody would likely even remember he was there. He made the turn into the almost hidden driveway and pressed the button on the remote control to open the big iron gate. They were home.

CHAPTER 5

Michael heard the phone on the other end ring four times before Bonnie Prescott picked up.

"Hello. Bonnie? This is Michael O'Conner, the private investigator that you visited yesterday. Are you still interested in pursuing a thorough probe into your brother's activities? I'm prepared to move ahead if you are."

"I'm anxious to get started," said Bonnie," what more do you need from me?"

Michael poised his pencil over the checklist on his desk. "First, I'll need the address of his place on the bay and the names of any of the neighbors that you might know. Do you know if he ever goes out to eat or just have a couple drinks? His favorite restaurants and bars?" He went on with several questions about the habits of Bonnie's brother and then waited for the answers. It didn't surprise Michael that Bonnie was unable to supply much more than the address. She didn't know any of the neighbors or how often her brother ate out. She did say that he had always had a fondness for an occasional Coor's Light at whatever tavern might be handy.

"Can you tell me anything about his years in college? Things like dates he attended and year of graduation? Any friends that he might have mentioned? How about a college yearbook?"

"Brian never owned a yearbook but there was one that my parents bought. They insisted that he carry it around on Graduation Day and collect a few autographs and memories. He wasn't too fond of the idea and I remember seeing it under my mother's arm when we left the campus. I found it after my parents died and I was cleaning up their house. I'm pretty sure I still have it somewhere. I'll find it for you. I don't recall that he ever mentioned anybody from school, maybe when I look at the yearbook it will jar my memory."

Michael signed off and went to work. He began by digging into Brian's local community, compiling lists of area realtors, hardware stores, restaurants, bars, and so on. With so little to go on and no concrete proof that anything illegal was taking place, Michael had to be careful about creating a situation that might spawn a libel suit or any other such nonsense. This would need to be a discreet investigation. As a matter of fact, if he wanted the desired results, it couldn't even look like an investigation.

But this was the kind of case that Michael had always dreamed about, a beautiful and desperate young woman in need of answers and willing to pay for them. He felt like Sam Spade.

The following morning, armed with a cash card and a generous retainer that Bonnie had dropped off, Michael hopped in his Trailblazer, threw his gear bag in the back seat and headed north. Before noon his GPS indicated that he was in front of the driveway to Brian Prescott's hideaway. He cruised by the barely discernable entrance to the driveway without slowing down and headed for Caseville, the next town to the north where he could get a bite to eat and establish his field office.

Spotting the free wi-fi sign out front he pulled into the motel parking lot and walked into the office where he paid for two nights in advance. The woman at the desk provided him with about a half dozen brochures spotlighting the local nightlife and fishing charters.

Michael had cropped the old photo of Brian Prescott and blown it up as big as he could without it becoming too grainy. There were eight copies in his notebook. He was satisfied that he could recognize the man if he ran across him. There were a number of restaurants and bars in town but that would be too much like looking for a needle in a haystack. He decided to start with the local police chief. Otis Springfield had given him an introduction and he seemed mildly intrigued with Michael's investigation.

The first thing the following morning, Michael found his way to the village hall. A sign on the lawn said. "Police Department – rear entrance." Chief Gallagher was almost just the way Michael had pictured him—tall, fit, and suntanned. The only thing missing was the hair. The chief didn't have one of those shaved heads, he was just bald. Michael hoped he hadn't been caught staring but the guy sure sounded like he had hair when they talked on the phone.

"C'mon in and have a chair. Getcha a coffee or anything?" The chief was warming up his own brew from a pot on the credenza behind his metal desk. A row of coffee mugs with the village logo lined the windowsill above the coffee pot.

"I'm fine," replied Michael as he sank into the chair. He dug out a copy of the mug shot of Brian Prescott and pushed it across the desk.

"Oh, I know who he is. I've never actually met the guy but I've seen him around town. I remember his grandparents. They were really good people but everybody tells me that Brian was bad news when he was a young teenager. I guess he used to spend part of his summers with his grandparents. Back then, they still had neighbors and he was always picking on their kids for no reason. Nothing that ever resulted in police involvement though, just being a mean kid. Finally he went away to college and while he was gone everything changed. All of the neighbors moved away by then and Old Man Prescott started buying up all the property. He died a couple of years later and his wife hung on for another couple of years or so. She's gone too."

"And now the grandson owns it all."

"That's the story but I haven't heard of any problems down that way. It's not exactly in my jurisdiction but I would have heard if it had become a special attention situation. Everything's been quiet since he took the place over." The chief slid into the chair behind his desk and looked at the photo for a few seconds. "This looks like an old picture but he still looks pretty much the same."

Michael opened his notebook and pulled a ballpoint out of his shirt pocket. "It seems that Brian's twin sister is convinced he's up to no good. In fact she's pretty sure of it. She hired me to investigate the situation."

"Yeah, your buddy Lieutenant Springfield filled me in. That property isn't part of any incorporated community but I know the County Deputy who patrols that stretch of road. I can ask him if he's heard anything. He's a local guy who grew up right in that area and he knows absolutely everybody."

"That's the kind of connection I was hoping for," replied Michael. "Is there any chance that I can talk to him?"

"I'm sure he'd be glad to help, he's a really conscientious guy. Can I have him call you?"

Michael recited his cell phone number, thanked the chief and headed to one of the local establishments for lunch. He had decided to dine in places that served beer so that he could check out anybody who happened to be drinking a Coor's Light.

CHAPTER 6

Every resort town seems to have a segment of its population that doesn't appear to understand that almost their entire existence is dependent on the tourist trade. Business owners certainly recognize it. Main Street is saturated with gift and souvenir shops while there's not a single accounting firm or law office in sight. But there are those who resent the intrusion of vacationers and do everything they can to make them feel unwelcome. Michael encountered one of these on his first visit to a local restaurant.

Butch's Food and Spirits was housed in an old building around the corner from the brightly painted tourist traps. By comparison the place looked shabby but it wasn't really that bad. It was the kind of place where the locals hung out. A good bowl of chili and a cold beer kind of joint.

Michael had grabbed a local newspaper from the stand out front and was scanning it at a table under one of the dozen or so ceiling fans that provided the small town version of air conditioning.

A scrawny guy with wire rimmed glasses and neatly combed short brown hair was sitting at the lunch counter with his back to Michael. He kept looking over his shoulder and Michael could feel his eyes. He finally stood up and swaggered over to Michael's table. The name embroidered on his work uniform shirt identified him as "Driller."

"You're not from around here."

Michael didn't answer. He merely shook his head slowly and continued to bury his nose in the newspaper.

The man became irritated. "Then why you readin' the town newspaper? You don't know anybody in it."

Michael lowered the paper and looked the man in the eye. "Is there something I can do for you?"

Driller leaned forward and placed both hands on the table. "You're one of them flatlanders."

Michael relaxed a little realizing that this guy was no threat. Leaning forward and supporting himself on the table, he was in no position to launch a physical attack. Conversely, he was in a quite vulnerable posture if Michael had been inclined to take a swipe at him. "Look mister, I'm just in here for a bowl of soup. I'm sorry that you don't like it but it's a public restaurant."

A female voice from behind the counter yelled, "Driller, get your ass over here and sit down. Quit botherin' the customers."

Driller slowly rose to his full height of 5 feet, 7 inches as Michael held his gaze like a fighter plane locked on to its target. Finally Driller blinked. Defeated, he returned to his stool at the lunch counter but now everybody in the place had taken a long hard look at the stranger in town. Michael's anonymity had been compromised.

The waitress brought Michael his soup and sandwich. "Sorry about that guy. He owns a local well drilling business. You'd think he'd know better. He makes most of his money putting in wells for summer cottages all along the waterfront. He'll never light a candle because he gets way too much satisfaction out of cursing the darkness. Some people don't understand that without tourists we'd still have dirt roads out there. If they want to keep everything to themselves, they should move to one of the inland towns instead of right here on the beach. Hell, they never even go in the water anyway."

Michael smiled at the waitress, "No harm done. Everybody's entitled to their opinion."

"You don't look like you're on vacation though. You're wearing slacks and shoes n' socks. Most of the guys are in shorts and flip-flops."

Michael laughed, "I guess you could say I'm here on business."

"What kind of business?" Driller, a scowl on his face had turned his stool around and was looking at Michael again.

Without missing a beat, Michael fired back, I'm with a major well drilling corporation. We're looking for new markets for our state of the art techniques. We can drill deeper wells in half the time and half the cost of conventional methods. That's why I was reading the newspaper. I'm looking for a piece of property to build our new facility." Michael winked at the waitress. She smiled and walked back to the kitchen and Michael finished his meal in a silence only occasionally interrupted by a sneezing fit that seemed to have possessed Driller. On his way out the door Michael dropped his folded newspaper on the counter top in front of Driller. "Here, I'm done with it. There's a cool article in there about a guy that sneezed so hard that he damaged a spinal nerve and was paralyzed." Michael walked away and Driller suppressed a sneeze, stared at the newspaper, afraid to touch it and pondering the probability of spending the rest of his life in a wheelchair.

Not a single person at Butch's Food and Spirits had been drinking a Coor's Light but then nobody there had resembled the photograph of Brian Prescott. Michael pulled out of the parking lot and headed south for another look at the wooded hideaway where Brian was presumably plotting his war on mankind. Along the way, his cell phone rang. He didn't recognize the number but the incoming call was coming from the local area code. His answer was brief. "O'Conner Investigations. Michael O'Conner speaking."

"Hello, this is Deputy Waldecker, Huron County Sheriff's Department. Chief Gallagher said you needed some information."

"Well, I've been hired by a woman who has concerns about what her brother could be up to and the Chief told me that you might be willing to help."

Deputy Waldecker didn't hesitate, "You got a GPS?"

"Yes, sir."

The deputy rattled off an address, "Put this in your unit and meet me there at one o'clock. Can you make it?"

Michael quickly loaded the address and the GPS told him that he was about twenty minutes away. "Looks good from my end."

"Great. See you there."

CHAPTER 7

The building was an early 1900s township hall. Two cars were parked out front, a Ford Taurus and a County Sheriff's cruiser. Michael wheeled his Trailblazer into one of the several empty spots in the lot.

"You must be O'Conner," the young man in the crisp uniform extended his hand.

Michael was surprised at how young the guy looked but the cluster of ribbons on the man's chest testified to some time in the uniform. He was tall and muscular like a college athlete and he radiated confidence. His intelligent eyes completed the package. "That would be me," Michael replied with a grin.

The deputy led Michael into a small cubicle that was wrapped around a desk and two chairs. The absence of anything on the desk gave it an unassigned look. The two men sat down. "I actually know the guy you're investigating. Or at least I knew him a little bit when he was a kid. Knew his sister too but I doubt if either one would remember me. I was just one of the local brats who hung out around the ice cream stand in town. They were about two or three years older than me so had nothing to do with me. Two years is a lot when you're thirteen." Waldecker laughed.

"I see," said O'Conner. "Do you remember what he was like back then? You do know that Brian is living here full-time, right?"

"Brian was always a hard guy to figure out. He didn't seem to do much with the other guys. He mostly kept to himself and just watched whatever was going on. Never said much. I've only seen him a few times since he's lived here though. Saw him coming out of his driveway in his black Dodge Durango about a month ago. Wrote down his license number just in case. I know that he's considered a weirdo."

"Have there been any complaints? I know that he doesn't have any neighbors close by but I was wondering if he's ever bothered anyone. Or maybe he might have called the police if he had a trespasser. I hear he likes his privacy."

"Nope, there's never been any reason to pay him a visit. I pulled into his driveway once but there's a barrier gate a little ways inside so I backed out. Haven't been back since."

Michael cleared his throat. "His sister is convinced that he's up to no good. She's sure that he's planning something big. Something that's going to hurt people."

"Well, I don't trust him either so I've put my neighborhood snoop network to work. About the only thing that I've come up with is that he never hangs out in the tourist bars or restaurants although he has been seen two or three times in a little beach restaurant down at the public bathing beach. He goes in to some of the off-strip taverns from time to time but hardly talks to anyone. Another one of my snitches tells me that he's been seen a few times at a place called Miller's Bar in Bay City. Seems like that's kind of a long way to go for a beer, it's about an hour drive from here. He must have some other sort of reason for going down there."

Michael was scribbling in his notebook. "Sure would be nice to get a good look at the place. Seems like you should be able to see it from the bay."

"Already thought of that. I didn't want to use the department's boat so I bribed one of my buddies with a six pack of Killian's Red to take me by there in his 20' Sea Ray. I had binoculars and a camera with a big telephoto but didn't find anything worth worrying about. Looks like he's been working on one of the trawlers and the old drag link is still floating on its barge at the dock. It appears that there are a few new pilings holding the docks in place. Nothing to get too suspicious about, just general fix-up stuff."

"Have you ever seen the place from the air?"

Deputy Waldecker scratched his head. "I haven't but our department has a plane and a helicopter. We've usually got to have some good reason to use them but every so often we're required to take them up for check-out and some of the guys tag along just for the hell of it. I'll find out when the next audit flight is coming up and maybe you and I can go for a ride.

Michael was surprised at the invitation. "You can take civilians up?"

"I'm not sure just what the policy says but I know that I do it all the time. If there's anything coming up soon, I think that I can pull the right strings. I'll let you know."

Michael closed his notebook. "You do it? Are you the pilot?"

"I'm one of them, actually I'm the senior pilot for both

the airplane and the helicopter." Waldecker pointed to the wings pinned to his uniform.

"Looks like I'm talking to the right guy then," commented Michael.

"Right, I'm not just another pretty face," said the deputy. "I'm also the water search and rescue coordinator."

Michael whistled and reached across the desk to shake the deputy's hand before leaving for Bay City to check out Miller's Bar. Deputy Waldecker was right. Brian must have a good reason for driving an hour just for a cold beer.

CHAPTER 8

"Good morning, Shorty. Did you sleep well?"

"Sure did. Them six Budweisers helped a little. But I'm up and ready to go to work."

Brian waved Shorty out of his doorway and headed down to the dock where the 48 foot wooden trawler was tied up. "Here's where it begins."

Shorty momentarily looked awestruck. "Wow, mister. You weren't kidding about it being a fishing boat, were you? That's a serious-looking piece of equipment. What sort of work does it need?"

"Well, you can start by cleaning it up from end to end. I like things to sparkle a little bit. I figure that it will take at least three weeks or more to get that done. I'd suggest that you start in the engine compartments. I've got all the cleaning supplies that you should need in that big shed at the end of the dock. I'll let you set your own hours but I'll be expecting no less than eight hours a day from you. You can work as much as you want and I pay time-and-a-half after forty hours and double time on Sundays."

Brian was pleased to see the wheels turning once again in Shorty's head. He was pretty sure that Shorty wasn't smart enough to estimate his potential fortune without a calculator, but he could tell that the little man envisioned a wonderful future.

"Can I go on the clock right now?" asked Shorty.

"Sure, consider yourself working right now. But why don't you come up to the house for breakfast first and we can chat a little bit about everything that I'll be needing."

Shorty smiled. "Lead the way, boss."

The house was a large Victorian estate. It looked old but everything about it smelled brand new. It was an imposing structure and way too big for one person. The kitchen was especially impressive; it looked like the set on one of those television cooking shows.

Brian had already prepared a plate full of sausages and warmed them in the microwave while he quickly scrambled a half dozen eggs. A fresh pot of coffee sat on the countertop. As soon as the toaster popped, breakfast was ready.

"We're sure way off the beaten path back here, ain't we?" Shorty wiped his mouth with a linen napkin. "I mean, I can't even hear the cars going by out on the road. How far back are we anyways?"

"Little over a quarter mile as near as I can figure. I guess it was a little too swampy for them when they first built the highway out there so they kept their distance from the shoreline. Ground's pretty solid though. Never had a problem and this property has been in my family for over sixty years."

Shorty nodded. "So you're a commercial fisherman, are ya?"

"No, that's way too much work for me. That was my grandfather's gig. I just want to fix up the boat and other stuff so that I can sell it. I'm getting the place ready to be my retirement home."

"Okay. So I'm gonna start by cleaning up that old fishing tug out there and then what?"

Brian leaned back in his chair. "Well, then there's the barge and dredging equipment. That's going to have to look real good so that I can get a decent price for it. That job should last into September or so and then I'll want to do some upgrading on the rest of the place. You know, all of the storage sheds and the dock. Things like that. I can also use a maintenance guy to take care of the lawn and stuff."

"And that old boathouse too, right?"

"For now, you can just forget about that boathouse. Eventually I'm going to buy a bubbling apparatus for that so that I can store a boat in the water year round. The boathouse is over 60 feet deep and 25 feet wide. I'll be able to store a good size pleasure boat in there some day. But right now there's no reason for you to even go near it so you can forget that it's even there." Brian paused for a moment. "Understand?"

Shorty didn't respond, he simply nodded his head.

After breakfast, Brian showed Shorty where to find all of the cleaning supplies and led him out to the trawler. He said. "You can break for lunch around noon. Just come up to the house and let yourself in. There will be something to eat in the kitchen."

Without another word Shorty climbed aboard and immediately disappeared below the deck.

Brian wandered over to the massive boathouse and unlocked the padlock that hung on the pedestrian door. When he turned on the lights, dorsal fins began to break the surface of the water. The fish knew that it was feeding time. Brian walked over to the walk-in cooler and pulled a fresh ham off of one of the hooks. He carried the twenty pound cut of meat over to the indoor dock and threw it into the water. The sharks circled it for a minute or two and then the first one hit it hard and shook a large piece of meat loose. The others quickly converged on what was left. Brian walked back over to the cooler, grabbed another large ham and repeated the process. Now the water was boiling in a feeding frenzy. Brian watched for a few moments seemingly mesmerized. He was envisioning Shorty in the middle of that frantic school of flesh-eating fish, screaming for his life. He knew that he'd have to act soon because he was getting to know Shorty and he didn't want to risk taking a liking to him. The fish would be satisfied today but they'd be hungry again tomorrow and if he made them wait for one additional day, they'd be famished and ready to attack anything. Brian smiled.

CHAPTER 9

"I'm trying to locate a long-lost family member for some folks downstate. There was a rumor that he comes in here from time to time." Michael pushed the photo across the surface of Miller's Bar in Bay City.

The bartender could have been a professional wrestler. His neck was the thickness of a fireplug and just about as ugly. Huge arms bulged under the denim shirt. He eyed Michael suspiciously without so much as glancing at the picture. The steroid swollen voice asked, "Why are you looking?"

Michael produced his Private Investigator identification card and said, "His sister is trying to find him. He's not in any kind of trouble. It's a personal matter."

The bartender slowly lowered his eyes and looked at the picture. "Coor's Light. Comes in once in a while, maybe once a week or so. Don't know his name but that's what he drinks. He was just in here a couple of nights ago. Kept pretty much to himself, had a couple of beers and then left. Two-dollar tip."

"Does he usually talk to anybody while he's here?"

The bartender stroked his dark goatee. "Once in a while he might make a comment but I've never seen him in a conversation with anybody. Doesn't have any friends in here."

"Excuse me." The request came from a short, chubby lady with a short flat hairdo combed straight back. She wore a clean and neatly ironed floral print housedress and high-top tennis shoes. She could generously be described as plain but more accurately called homely. "I'm trying to locate my husband. I called here a couple of nights ago and talked to him. His name is Wallace Stueber. Most people just call him Shorty."

The bartender surveyed the sad-looking woman. "So you're Shorty's wife? He's been coming in here for at least three years off and on and I never even knew he was married."

"He don't always tell everybody, he's kind of a private guy. Have you seen him in the last couple of days? I'm getting worried. I haven't heard anything from him since he said that he found a job somewhere up north on a fishing boat. He doesn't always come home at night but he usually calls so that I don't worry about him. He don't have a cell phone or nothing so he's always got to borrow one or find a pay phone." The woman looked extremely distraught.

"Nope. He was in here playing Keno and he had a winning ticket. Took off right after that and I ain't seen him since."

"Well, if he comes in, make sure you tell him to call me. I haven't slept in two nights." The woman turned and shuffled toward the door, sobbing softly.

As soon as the woman was out of earshot the bartender laughed and turned back to Michael. "She's certainly no prize. But neither is that little creep, Shorty. They look like a good match."

"Was Shorty in the bar the same time this guy was?"

Michael tapped his finger on the picture of Brian Prescott that was still sitting on the bar.

"Now that you mention it, I'm pretty sure he was. If I remember correctly, they both left about the same time."

Michael threw a ten on the bar, snatched up the picture, said thanks and hurried out the door to catch the woman who had just left. He saw her across the street climbing into an extremely rusty Ford Ranger pickup truck. "Oh lady," he yelled, "May I ask you a couple of questions?"

The woman stopped with the door open and one foot in the truck. "Are you a cop?" she asked.

"No, no, nothing like that but I'm a private investigator looking for another man who was known to be in this bar about the same time your husband was." Michael already had his I.D. card in his hand. "The man that I'm gathering information on lives north of here and he owns a couple of big fishing boats. It's just possible that there's some kind of connection."

The woman stopped and seemed to consider Michael's words. "I just don't know where to turn. It's like I'm the only person in the world who cares about poor Shorty. Everybody laughs at me because I'm worried about him, like he don't matter. But he does. He's a good man; it's just that people don't ever take him serious. But I love him like crazy." The pathetic looking little woman burst into tears.

Michael reached out to comfort her. "Let's talk a little and see if it helps. We can sit in my car if you like, it has air conditioning."

The woman managed a weak smile and followed Michael to where his Trailblazer was parked. They climbed inside and he started the engine. Soon the passenger compartment had cooled to a comfortable temperature. "Suppose you begin by telling me about your husband and why you're so worried."

"Well, Shorty's never had a break in his life. He has no education and so nobody wants to hire him. He's a good worker when he's got a job but he has a little drinking problem. Not a real bad one. I mean he never shows up drunk at work or gets nasty when he drinks or nothing like that. But it's enough to cause some headaches sometimes 'cause he never stays on a job very long. Lucky thing that I've got a couple of good jobs. I clean houses for two different maid services. Both outfits say that I'm the best girl they got. I work about sixty-five, seventy hours some weeks and only twenty or so on others. It's kind of spotty sometimes. Shorty contributes whenever he can. We get by okay. He really sounded excited about this new job. Said it paid big money but he had to start right away, go up north immediately, couldn't even come home that night. He promised to call as soon as he could but I haven't heard a word."

"Has he ever done this kind of thing before?" Michael secretly hoped it was a normal behavior.

"Not like this. He usually has time to tell me what's going on and how much money he's gonna make. All he said the other night was that it was a fishing boat and it was up north somewhere. If he wanted the job, he was gonna have to ride up there with the boss right away. I don't know what to think."

"There's a chance that it was some kind of charter boat and they had to sail in the morning. He could be out on the water somewhere and can't get to a phone."

"I suppose that could be, but it's just not like him to leave me wondering like this. I'd feel so much better if he'd just call. I miss him so much. Don't you understand? He's all I have."

The desperation in her voice gave Michael chills. In spite of his attempts to reassure the woman, he had serious concerns for the welfare of her husband. There might be nothing to it, no connection at all between Shorty and Brian Prescott. But Michael couldn't shake the image of Brian's sister pleading with him to stop her brother before he wreaked havoc on an entire community. What started out as a simple fact-gathering day had left Michael emotionally exhausted.

CHAPTER 10

Michael's cell phone rang just as he pulled into his motel parking lot. It was Bonnie Prescott.

"I found Brian's college yearbook and it looks like there might be a little useful information in there."

"Great, what did you find?"

"Well I didn't recognize anybody in the book but there is one autograph, a strange name; Arunis Udrys. And there are also the names of a couple of the research vessels that he spent his summers on. One was called the Cheryl Ann out of Bar Harbor, Maine and the other was named Sweet Susie based in New Orleans. I guess that this Udrys guy served an internship on at least one of the boats with Brian."

Michael copied the information into his notebook. "That's good stuff. I'm sure that it will help."

"Have you found anything so far?" Her voice sounded anxious.

"Well, I've talked to the local police department and the sheriff's office and they both know who Brian is and they know why I'm here. And I've found at least one of the places that he's known to hang out in. Nothing more than that so far."

"That's sure a lot more than I could have uncovered. I'm feeling a lot better since you decided to take the case."

"I've got a sometimes partner down in the Detroit Police Department. He helps me out when he's off duty and I think he'll be free for the next couple of days. I'm going to pass on the yearbook information that you gave me and see what he can come up with."

"Will you keep me updated?"

"Of course, you're paying the bill and that makes you the boss."

It was the first time that Michael had heard Bonnie laugh. He thought it was a pretty laugh.

Detective McCoy answered on the first ring.

"Hey McCoy, you available for a couple of days?"

"Well, Mike, I'm not sure. There's a barstool over at Eddie's Bar with my name on it. Why, you got something interesting going on?"

"Yeah, I do. I'm up here in Caseville following up on leads for maybe two, three more days or I'd do it all myself. My client, Bonnie Prescott, found her brother's college yearbook and there's a possible connection to one of his classmates and some information about where and how he spent his summers. I guess he really was doing some sort of oceanic study during his vacations from school. Feel like checking any of it out?"

"Sure," answered McCoy, "I'll use your office so that the phone bill goes to you. Besides, it's air conditioned. How soon do you need answers?"

"I really don't know how urgent things are but I've got an uneasy feeling about a missing person up this way so I don't want to waste any time."

"I'll do the best I can," said McCoy. "Give me whatever information you can and I'll see what I can do."

Michael read the notes he'd taken from the conversation with Bonnie.

"Arunis Udrys shouldn't be too hard to find," chuckled McCoy. "I can't imagine that there are too many of them in the phone book."

"Unless he was a foreign student," speculated Michael, "It happens all the time in colleges."

It took McCoy exactly two hours to locate Arunis Udrys. He was now an employee of the Northeast Oceanic Institute working under the name Steven Udrees. He was not a faculty member but it was his job to set up field classes and make travel arrangements. He got the telephone number from the college directory.

There was a barely detectable European accent in the voice. "Northeast Oceanic, this is Steve. How may I help you?"

McCoy asked, "I'm trying to locate an Arunis Udrys?"

There was a long pause. "I am Arunis Udrys. Where did you get that name? I haven't used it in years."

"Oh, I apologize," said McCoy. "I got your name from Brian Prescott's college yearbook. Brian's sister is trying to locate him and you were the only contact we could find."

The man on the other end seemed to relax. "I haven't seen Brian since graduation. Can't say that I knew him very well anyway. We shared a couple of summer internships together but that's about it."

McCoy pressed on, "Do you have a little time to tell me about it? What kind of internships were they and maybe what Brian was interested in?"

"I'm sure that I won't be much help in locating him, it's been years."

"That's okay, we're trying to put together a little outline of his life so that we can figure out the best places to begin searching for him."

"We did a couple of summer studies together on some research vessels. The first year was up on the coast of New England where we studied the movement of several species of fish and then the next year we signed on to a boat down in the Gulf of Mexico. Brian was more active on that trip."

"Hmmm," McCoy mused, "What was so different about the southern trip?"

"Well, from what I remember the only difference was the kinds of fish we encountered. Brian was fascinated by the bull sharks. That whole summer cruise was focused on them. I never really understood why but he asked a million questions about them and read everything he could get his hands on. The only thing unique about them is that they thrive in fresh water, like up the Mississippi River and places like that but I'm sure you're not interested in hearing about fish."

"No problem," answered McCoy, "You never know which piece of information might help. Did you guys ever hang out together? Go bowling or anything like that?"

"The closest thing we ever did to socializing was a couple times when we had a beer together at a tavern near the dock in New Orleans. I remember him asking if we had any bull sharks back in Latvia."

"Latvia?"

"Yeah, that's where I was born. Roja, it's a coastal town. I never heard of any bull sharks in the Baltic."

McCoy laughed. "I guess that's enough for now. I'm going to give you my cell phone number and if you can think of anything else, no matter how insignificant it might seem I'd appreciate it if you'd call me."

"Okay but don't expect much. He was a pretty private guy."

McCoy read off his phone number and hung up.

CHAPTER 11

Brian was truly impressed with the amount of work Shorty had accomplished in his first couple of days. The starboard engine looked cleaner than he had ever imagined possible. The drip pan under the engine had been removed and polished and all of the bulkheads had been scrubbed to reveal their glossy grey finish. Several buckets full of soiled rags sat off to one side. The little man was drenched in sweat but smiling broadly as Brian inspected the progress. "Nice job, Shorty. If you do this well tomorrow, you'll have the hardest part behind you."

"I've had a lot tougher jobs over the years," responded Shorty, "I'll handle it. Might even be quicker because I learned a few shortcuts while I was working today." He was still grinning.

"Come on up to the house for dinner after you clean up. I picked up a half dozen new work uniforms and other stuff in your size while I was in town today so you can be nice and fresh. We're having lake perch tonight." Brian turned his back and headed toward the house.

The meal was delicious and filling. Shorty pushed himself back from the table. "Do you suppose it would be okay if I went into town for a couple of beers tonight?"

"I guess you could but there's plenty of beer in the refrigerator," said Brian.

"Yeah, I know, but I was wanting to play a little Keno so I'd need to find a bar somewhere."

Brian scratched his chin. "The only problem I have is that there are a few guys in town who wanted the job that you've got and I don't want them to know that I gave it to someone else. Can I trust you to keep quiet about where you work?"

"Oh, hell yes," laughed Shorty. "I never tell anybody my business. You got no problems there, mister."

"I suppose I could drive you into town and drop you off for a few hours. I've got a few things to pick up anyway. You're sure you can keep quiet about this place, right? I don't want any hard feelings among the natives."

"You got it, boss. My lips are sealed. Except to inhale a Budweiser or two." They both laughed.

It was a little after seven o'clock when Brian dropped Shorty off in front of Butch's Food & Spirits. Shorty was flush with the first three hundred in wages in his pocket. "You've got a big day ahead of you tomorrow. I'd better pick you up no later than eleven"

As Shorty got out of the car he said, "Ten-thirty if you like, I'm not that much of a night owl."

Brian nodded and drove off. Thoughts of Shorty and his sincere effort to please and impress troubled Brian as he drove back toward his home. He had picked up Shorty for the sole purpose of sacrificing him to the sharks and now he felt as if he was betraying a trust. Brian saw his mistake as giving Shorty a few days to live because now he was actually feeling a little sorry for him and becoming attached to him. But there would be no turning back. He couldn't allow Shorty to destroy his plans. The things that

Shorty had seen up to this point could easily add up to clues that might implicate Brian after his scheme is launched. No question, the man would have to die. And the sooner the better.

Shorty was just settling into his barstool when a nasal voice called out to him. "Hey, Shorty. Probably want your old job back, don't ya. Well, you ain't gonna get it. I don't need no rats working for me."

It was Driller, the loudmouth who owned the well drilling company and he was getting a good head start on a night of power-drinking. Shorty had no use for Driller. The man had fired him a couple of years ago when Driller tried to charge a client for drilling a 120 foot deep well when he had only gone down 100 feet and Shorty tipped off the customer.

Shorty tried to ignore him but Driller kept hurling insults across the bar. Finally he went over to Driller and said. "Look, I don't need anything from you. I've got a job and it's better than anything that you ever offered. I work for a real boss with real money, so get off my back."

Shorty went back to his barstool and began filling out Keno wager slips. He was here for a little enjoyment and wasn't interested in arguing. He figured that he had about three hours before the boss picked him up and so he was rationing out his money, between drinking and gambling. Within an hour his numbers came in, paying him two hundred and twenty dollars. "Yahoo," he hollered as he read the numbers on the Keno screen.

Across the room, Driller turned his head from the ball game on the big screen television. He didn't like it when Shorty succeeded at anything. He began to launch another verbal tirade while Shorty did his best to ignore him. Finally Shorty wearied of Driller's rant and wandered over to his tormentor's table and sat down.

"Look, Driller. I got no beef with you. Why can't you just leave me alone and let me enjoy myself?"

"You screwed me when you worked for me and I don't like being screwed." replied Driller.

"That's not the way I look at it. I was just trying to be honest with a customer. You were the one lying. Besides, that was over two years ago. Why can't we just call a truce?"

Driller looked away from Shorty and ran his fingers through his hair. "What kind of a job you got now?"

"I'm just doing some maintenance work for a private party, but it pays good and it looks like it's got a future."

Driller turned back to face Shorty. "Who's the private party, one of those millionaires out on Sand Point?"

Shorty shook his head. "It ain't one of those Sand Point places. I'm not supposed to talk about it. He's a really private guy and doesn't want everybody knowing his business."

"You and your damned secrets. You probably think I'm going to talk to your boss and try to get you fired."

"I'm not worried about you, Driller. I let my work speak for itself. I've got a job and I'm planning on keeping it."

Shorty got up from the table and stepped outside the door looking for a breath of fresh air. Looking across the road, he noticed a pay phone in the parking lot of a liquor store. He strolled over and dialed his home number.

When he returned to the tavern, Driller was nowhere to be seen. Shorty spent the next hour and a half drinking draft Budweiser and alternately winning and losing at Keno. He was actually still quite a bit ahead of the game. So far it had been a good night. Hearing his name, he looked up to see Brian Prescott standing by the door. He picked up his change and hurried out to the waiting Durango.

As they pulled away from the curb, a Chevy pick-up truck turned on its headlights about a half block back and settled in at a comfortable distance behind them as Brian and Shorty headed south.

CHAPTER 12

Michael wasn't sure whether or not he should feel relieved. Sharon Stueber had called him this morning to tell him that she'd heard from her husband. Her voice was perky.

"Shorty got ahold of me last night. He said that he's got this really great job doing maintenance on a huge fishing boat. He says it's got two big diesel engines and it's big enough for a crew of at least six. He's getting the boat ready to sail but he isn't sure if he'll be aboard when it goes out in the bay. He says that the guy has a whole bunch of other equipment that needs attention too. It looks like a good long job, maybe even permanent."

"Did he give you the name of the guy he's working for?"

"You know, I was just so excited to hear his voice that I didn't even think to ask. All I know is that it's somewhere up on Saginaw Bay on the thumb side."

In Michael's mind it all seemed to fit, Brian Prescott lived in the very area that Sharon Stueber had just described and he owned a large fishing trawler that hadn't seen service in close to a decade and would most certainly need plenty of fixing up if it was to ever return to open water.

"Mrs. Stueber, I'd appreciate it if you'd keep me up to date on anything you hear from your husband. I don't mean to alarm you but I have reason to believe that the man your husband is working for may be of interest to law enforcement. If you talk to him again, see if you can get his employer's name. As I said the last time we talked, there may be absolutely nothing to worry about but I'd like to be sure."

"Shorty sounded just fine. He didn't seem worried about nothing and he has sort of a sixth sense when it comes to trouble. But I'll ask him a few questions if you want."

"Just see if you can get the name of his employer. I'd like to talk to him if I could. Can you pass my number on to him?" Michael said goodbye and hung up.

His next call was from Detective McCoy who communicated all the information that he'd gleaned from Brian's old classmate. McCoy emphasized the interest that Brian had shown in bull sharks and their apparent ability to thrive in fresh water.

"My detective's head says that when a guy is a lot more than just casually interested in fierce and malicious fish, he has an isolated facility on a popular sports lake, and somebody thinks he's psychotic, I'd wanna closer look at what's going on in there."

Michael laughed at the notion. "Wouldn't that be something? That would be quite a stretch but I'm with you on wanting to get inside and see what's happening behind that barrier gate. I sure wish that we had some reasonable cause to pay him a personal visit but so far the only thing we have is the general consensus that the guy's a screwball who likes his privacy. Last I heard, they won't issue search warrants on those grounds."

McCoy changed direction. "How have the locals been

to work with? They cooperating or fighting you? I've heard that they're usually pretty helpful."

"Oh, they've been great," replied Michael, "They're even trying to make arrangements for an unofficial fly over in the County Sheriff's airplane so we can see what it looks like from the air. I can't ask them for an investigation because there hasn't been a crime or even a complaint. I'm going to try for a few pictures from offshore too. I brought my super powerful telephoto lens along."

McCoy responded. "I'm not sure how much you'll be able to see from out in the bay or up in the sky but it looks like those are your best options at the moment. How long you planning to hang around up there? I just started on a fourteen-day furlough and just might want to join you. The kind of investigating that you're doing is a detective's dream; only one case and nobody hanging over your shoulder telling you that there are more important things on your plate."

"I was originally planning to just be up here for a couple of days but as long as I'm making some kind of progress, I'll probably hang around. I didn't bring a lot of clothes along but there's a laundromat in town and I'm even making friends with some of the natives. If you come up here I'll introduce you to Driller."

McCoy laughed. "Seriously, if you're gonna be there for a week or so you might want to contact your client and see if she's willing to pop for another set of eyes."

"I can do that," replied Michael. "As a matter of fact it's not a bad idea at all. I won't say that I'm over my head in this investigation but it's looking more complicated every day. I could really use a guy with your experience."

As soon as Michael broke off his conversation with McCoy, he dialed Bonnie Prescott's number and brought her up to speed on everything that he knew so far. He also asked a couple of questions about the fishing trawler that was moored at Brian's dock and finally broached the subject of adding a second detective to the case. To Michael's surprise, Bonnie greeted his suggestion with enthusiasm.

"If you think another man on the team will help, I'm all for it. I'm actually amazed at how far you've gone already. You probably know more about Brian than anybody in the world besides me and in some areas, you're way ahead of me. Keep going, by all means. If he's hiding anything, it sounds like you're on the right path to find it. You have an open checkbook. Go for it."

"The guy I've got in mind is a Detroit cop and a real good one. I'll give you his phone number so that you can check him out for yourself."

"Sounds great," responded Bonnie.

As soon as Michael finished talking to Bonnie Prescott, his cell phone rang.

"Hello, O'Conner here."

"Hi Michael, this is Deputy Waldecker with the Sheriff's Department. Just wanted you to know that I'll be getting together for breakfast with Chief Gallagher from the Caseville Police Department. He suggested that I invite you along. I guess he's an old buddy of some friend of yours down at the Detroit P.D. and he's really curious to see what you're up to."

"Just tell me where and when and I'll be there. Oh, and breakfast will be on my client." Michael jotted down the information and signed off. He dialed McCoy's number to let him know he was now part of the investigating team and invited him to join the breakfast meeting with his new cop friends in the morning.

CHAPTER 13

Brian watched as Shorty lay on his belly scrubbing the aluminum drip pan under the big diesel engine. Although he didn't like admitting it, he was beginning to actually like the hardworking little man. Shorty couldn't have weighed more than 110 pounds by Brian's estimate but he labored like a man with a mission. Brian was almost sorry that he hadn't killed Shorty on his first night here. The sharks hadn't been fed on a regular basis in close to a week and were ready for a big meal. But Brian had caved in and fed them a couple of huge hams just two days ago and then nothing yesterday. They might just be hungry enough right now to attack fresh prey in the water. Brian knew that if he could put off feeding them for another day, the sharks would really build their appetites. In the meantime he'd get as much work out of Shorty as he could and try to distance himself as much as possible so that he wouldn't feel any remorse when the time came.

"What did you do in the bar last night?" queried Brian.

"Not much of anything really," replied Shorty, "Drank a few Budweisers and played a little Keno. Y'know, I'm beginning to think I'm addicted to that game. I should get away from it for a while. It just takes all my money." He didn't mention that he was still almost two hundred dollars ahead of the game.

"I know what you mean. It's probably better to just kick back with a few beers and tell bad jokes with all your drinking buddies. You know anybody around here?" asked Brian.

"Me and some of my buddies used to come to the beach here when I was a teenager but that was a long time ago. I never had any friends or relatives who lived around here though."

Brian seemed pleased with Shorty's answer. "Okay, I'll let you get back to work. I've got to run into town for a few things. Be back in a couple of hours."

Brian pulled out of his driveway after waiting for a slow-moving Chevy pickup truck to pass. The driver of the truck seemed to be craning his neck to get a good look at him. "What's your problem, dude?" muttered Brian as he turned north on the highway.

Shorty pulled himself up from the lower deck of the trawler. He was almost done cleaning things up but nature was calling. Rather than head back to his little shack, he decided to relieve himself into the bay. He knew that nobody was around but just the same, he walked a few dozen yards down the dock to where it hugged the wall of the in-water boat house. At first he thought it was just the sound of the gentle waves hitting the wooden walls of the boathouse but after a few minutes he realized that the splashing sound was coming from inside the boathouse. As he leaned around the edge to have a look at the front, he noticed what looked like an underwater gate across the entrance. It was a formidable-looking fabrication that looked like it could withstand a direct hit from a torpedo. His curiosity finally got the best of him and he went around the side of the boathouse where he found an unlocked window. It took a bit of coaxing but it finally slid up and gave him plenty of room to climb through.

The well inside of the boathouse was big enough for at least a 50 foot boat with a 16 foot beam. Maybe even bigger. There was a narrow walkway on one side of the boat well and a wide one on the other. There was a large dock at the back that must have been at least 15 feet deep. A forklift truck was parked just inside a rear access door. Three rows of large storage bins full of old fishing nets were stacked almost to the ceiling against the back wall. Not much light found its way through the solitary window but Shorty could still make out a lot of activity in the large pen in front of him. Given the amount of noise and turbulence, the fish stirring restlessly in circles had to be extremely large. He was about to search for a light switch when a shadow flitted past the open window. Shorty knew that he wasn't supposed to be in the boathouse but the only way out was the window and he was sure to be caught if he tried to exit there. He looked for a place to hide. The only area that offered any concealment was the dozens of baskets at the back wall. Shorty squeezed between a couple of them and found enough space behind the first row to hunker down and peer through the narrow space between them. He was far enough back in the shadow that he felt relatively safe. His eyes had become fairly well accustomed to the dim light and he could clearly see the familiar form of a man crawling through the window.

"Hey, Shorty. I know you're in here. Where're ya hidin'?" The man had his hands on his hips and was struggling to see even a few feet in front of him.

Shorty realized that it wasn't Brian out there, it was that jerk, Driller. He must have followed Brian's Durango home from the bar the other night. Shorty didn't respond. As a matter of fact he didn't even breathe. He had no idea why Driller had followed him or why he couldn't let things go, but Shorty knew that a creep like that was bad news. He remained totally motionless.

Driller moved slowly down the walkway toward the dock where Shorty was hiding. He had one hand on the wall feeling his way. It was then that the commotion in the water grabbed his attention. "What the hell? You swimmin' in there, Shorty?" His next step caught the edge of the dock. He stumbled and splashed into the boat well. At first he attempted to simply tread water while he tried to catch his breath. Then something bumped him hard sending him out to the center of the well. A searing pain shot through his left thigh and at the same time he felt his right arm being ripped from his body. They were all on him at once. His shrieks inside the boathouse were deafening and the water around him began to boil.

Shorty was in total shock and couldn't watch any more, his eyes were tightly shut and his hands pressed hard over his ears. He was crying uncontrollably as a human being was being ripped to shreds just a few yards away. He felt as if he had caused Driller's death although he knew that there was nothing he could have done to prevent it. The screaming stopped and eventually the thrashing in the water began to subside. Shorty still couldn't move. He was frozen with fear. What had he discovered? Why was this boathouse filled with man-eating fish? They must be sharks. What else could they be? Sharks? In Saginaw Bay?

How is that possible? Sharks live in the ocean in salt water, not fresh.

Shorty lay on the rough dock for what seemed like hours, drifting in and out of reality trying to understand just what was happening.

Suddenly he was alert. A car door slammed somewhere in the distance. It had to be Brian. It was too late to run now. He'd have to remain where he was. He could only hope that he wouldn't be found.

CHAPTER 14

One of the more interesting of the over three hundred and seventy-five known shark species is the *Carcharhinus Leucs* or more commonly known as the bull shark. As sharks go they're not the biggest, averaging only about 7.5 to maybe 8 feet long and 285 pounds although some females have measured as much as 11 feet or more and weighed in at well over 500 pounds. But they're quite different from other sharks.

Shark attacks on humans are generally attributed to only three species; the Great White, the Tiger, and the Bull. Among them, bull sharks account for the greatest amount of attacks on humans primarily because they prefer the shallow waters where people swim. With the highest testosterone level of any living creature, they're considered aggressive predators and they're totally fearless. These creatures have the ability to sense even the most minute movements of their prey at great distances in extremely cloudy water. They're one of the few shark species known to be willing to take on extremely large prey.

What sets bull sharks apart from the others is their ability to tolerate and even thrive in fresh water. Scientists surmise that this evolutionary phenomenon may be simply the result of following the food chain or perhaps so that their young might have a higher survival rate away from the larger predators. But the science community admits that it doesn't really understand why they leave the clear ocean for the sometimes murky waters of freshwater lakes and rivers. Bull sharks are an established inhabitant of Lake Nicaragua, a freshwater lake in Central America and they are also known to permeate the waters over 2500 miles up the Amazon River. Bull sharks have been found in the Mississippi River as far north as Illinois and although there is some question about how it got there, there was a dead bull shark recovered in northern Lake Michigan near Traverse City, Michigan.

All sharks need salt or some of their cells will rupture causing bloating and death. But the bull shark has unique glands near its tail that retain salt and their kidneys have the ability to recycle the salt in their systems.

Brian Prescott had spent a lot of time studying bull sharks in college. To other students they may have held a fascination because of their place in the evolutionary cycle but Brian had a much more utilitarian purpose in mind.

The lower peninsula of the state of Michigan resembles a mitten and the thumb of that mitten forms the eastern shore of Saginaw Bay. The water rushing from the upper lakes runs deep into the bay where it collides with the quick flow of the Saginaw River at the base of the bay as well as several smaller tributaries that feed the large bay from various points up and down the shoreline. The result is a swirling tide that works its way up the inner edge of the thumb until it can spill over into Lake Huron. The lone obstacle is Sand Point, a peninsula near the tip of the thumb that extends about five and a half miles out into the bay. Here the water has to make a western detour to join the main body of the lake. Below that point is an area known as Wildfowl Bay, once home to a number of commercial fisheries. Now it is mainly a waterfowl refuge. Unlike the rest of the bay with its sandy bottom, it's near-shore waters sit on a pretty much murky environment overgrown with swamp-grass and cattails. By Great Lakes standards Saginaw Bay is quite shallow, averaging somewhere around 50 feet deep. The summer sun warms the bay to very comfortable temperatures. It's also the perfect environment for bull sharks.

CHAPTER 15

Brian stood inside the boathouse staring at the debris floating in the water; a tennis shoe, a part of a pant leg, and a few scraps of what may have been a tee shirt. There were still traces of blood in the water. The sharks were slowly milling just below the surface. He sighed. "I told you not to come in here. It's your own fault, you dumb little bastard. If you'd have just done your job and kept your nose out of things that don't concern you, I would have let you live at least a little while longer."

Shorty froze when he heard those words. Let who live a little while longer? Me? Is this what you had planned for me all along? He shrunk closer to the planks of the dock as if trying to make himself invisible. Brian walked back and forth in the boathouse his voice rising with his mood. He was working himself into a crazed frenzy. Soon he was screaming about how Shorty had ruined everything and that he'd been warned not to come in here.

Shorty shuddered to think that it was only a matter of time before he'd be spotted. But after about fifteen minutes the light went out and he heard Brian snap the padlock on the outside of the pedestrian door. He didn't move a muscle for several minutes. He barely breathed. The only sound was the gentle swishing of the water as the sharks moved slowly in their pen. The sun would be setting soon and he hoped to escape in the darkness of night. Through a crack between the boards of the old boathouse Shorty could see the main house about a hundred and fifty yards away. From what he remembered about the layout, the living room and kitchen were on the opposite side of the building and those were the two rooms where Brian would most likely be spending his time. That was a break. He slowly dragged himself out of the cramped little space where he'd been hiding and now stood on one of the walkways that bordered the shark pen. He could see them clearly now, swimming and circling ever so slowly. They looked graceful and content. Shorty couldn't get over how big they seemed. No wonder Driller had screamed so much. It must have been a horrible way to die.

Through the window something caught his eye. Brian had come out of the house and was bounding down the front porch stairs. Shorty's first impulse was to dive back into his little sanctuary but as he watched he saw Brian change his course and head for his Durango. He vaulted into the seat and sped out of the driveway. It was a situation that Shorty hadn't expected. With Brian gone, he would have enough time to scramble across the dock to his little shack and retrieve a few things before hightailing it out of here.

Once he got into his quarters Shorty didn't waste any time. He grabbed his wallet with close to four hundred and fifty dollars in it, a small flashlight that actually belonged to Brian, and the three packs of Marlboros that sat on his dresser. He snatched his jacket off the back of a chair and headed for the driveway. He walked in the grass off to one side so that he'd avoid leaving footprints in the loose gravel. It would be best if Brian thought that the sharks had eaten him. Once he got to the electronic gate he veered off through the woods angling toward the highway. When he got within sight of the pavement he turned south following the road staying well back behind the tree line so that he couldn't be seen by passing traffic. It was almost dark now and the mosquitoes were attacking with a vengeance. Shorty wished he'd thought about stuffing a few of those insect repellant wipes in his pocket. When the sky was finally black he made his way out to the shoulder of the road where the walking would be easier. Every time he saw headlights approaching he would creep into the ditch and lie down until they passed. The timing worked out perfectly because he got to the small town of Bay Port at about 1:30 in the morning and there wasn't a living person to be seen. He was able to stay in the shadows and remain invisible as he worked his way through the tiny village. By the time the morning sun began to break the plane of the horizon he was well south of town, had found an abandoned hay barn and was curled into a fetal position in the corner of the mow, an old rotting tarp pulled over his body. He felt safe here.

It took him a long time to find sleep. The adrenaline was only beginning to subside and his mind still couldn't see any logic in the terrifying events of the past twelve hours. Why would anybody be keeping sharks in a boathouse? Was it illegal to raise sharks? He didn't think so but then why all the secrecy? And what about that remark about allowing him to live a little while longer? A little while? That's what was so was frightening. But then maybe he heard it wrong. Maybe that's not what Brian said at all...

but that's what he heard. There was also the chance that the reason Brian left so quickly is that he was going to get the Sheriff to report the tragic accident. He just didn't know what was really happening but his survival instincts told him to stay out of anybody's reach until he had some credible answers.

His thoughts drifted back to the night he'd first encountered Brian. He felt as if something wasn't quite right from the very beginning. A complete stranger offering a loan should have sent up a red flag and then the offer of a high-dollar job from a guy that he'd only known for a few short words... that should have set off sirens. Now it was all making a little sense but there were still a million questions. Within the next five minutes his mind was finally eased by the onset of twelve hours of fitful slumber. When he awoke from his nightmare, it was still broad daylight and he was faced with the decision of whether to stay hidden in the relative safety of the old barn or to strike out walking and take a chance on being seen by Brian. He hadn't had anything to eat or drink for close to twenty-four hours and his body screamed for nourishment. He knew that he wasn't far from the village of Sebewaing and there would be restaurants there. It wouldn't be as dangerous if there were other people around. The chills began to creep back into his consciousness as he descended the old ladder from the hay mow. By the time he got to the doorway of the old barn he was almost paralyzed with fear. He stood back in the darkness for a long time scrutinizing the highway. Eventually he set out walking, trying to look as confident as he could. Within an hour he was in town and had taken to the side streets for a little more invisibility. Emerging from the residential street, he spotted a McDonald's restaurant just a couple of blocks away. That would be perfect, lots of people and a chance to satisfy his ravenous hunger.

Once inside, Shorty headed directly for the men's room to clean up a little and maybe comb his hair. He could still see the fear in his eyes when he looked in the mirror. After scrubbing his face, he opened the door slowly and scanned the entire crowd before returning to the restaurant. As he stood in the ordering line, consumed by his paranoia, his head was on a constant swivel watching for Brian to come storming through the door. He finally took a seat in a corner booth and wolfed down his burger and fries. It was then that he noticed a pay phone on the wall.

Shorty left the tray and food wrappers on the table and walked over to the phone. He dialed his home number and his wife Sharon picked up on the fourth ring. "Oh, it's so good to hear your voice. Do you like the new job? Can I come and visit?"

"Wait, wait," Shorty whispered into the phone. "Everything's turned to garbage. He's trying to kill me. Running for my life. I need you to come and get me."

Just then a black Dodge Durango wheeled into the parking lot. What felt like a high voltage electric shock ran though Shorty's entire body. His vision was going dark and he dropped the phone and ran out the back door of the restaurant. He didn't stop running until he was three blocks into the tree-lined streets of the quiet neighborhood. The warm weather had people out watering their lawns and tending their flowerbeds. He slowed to a walk and tried to blend in although he couldn't help feeling as if he stood out. No black Dodge Durango came down the street and he was the only pedestrian on the sidewalk. Maybe it hadn't been Brian after all but it sure looked like his silhouette behind the wheel. He adjusted his route to a southern heading and kept going. Soon it would be dark and he could walk all night. As he was exiting the southern edge of town he came across a sporting goods store. Ducking inside he made his way to the hiking and camping section. He had enough money to buy a small backpack, a two-man trail tent, a cheap light-weight sleeping bag, camp stove, a six pack of water bottles along with a handful of pre-prepared dehydrated meals and energy bars. He picked up a hunting knife and a compass as an afterthought.

He filled the water bottles at the spigot on the outside of the building, slipped them in the backpack and wound his way through the parking lot and back to the highway. There was still probably two hours of daylight and the thought of being seen terrified him but there was nothing he could do but push on. Soon the sun slid behind the cornfields and he was able to walk in relative safety.

CHAPTER 16

It was a bright and beautiful restaurant overlooking the harbor where very expensive yachts bobbed lazily in their slips. The tall masts of the sailboats swayed gently in the brilliant morning sunshine. Michael was the first to arrive and requested a table for five. The waitress escorted him to a seat in front of the big picture window and he lost himself in the beauty of the sparkling blue water of the bay as he waited for his coffee. He was surprised to see Bonnie Prescott arrive with McCoy.

"Wow, I didn't expect you," said an embarrassed Michael.

Bonnie just smiled. "It was his idea," she said as she tilted her head toward McCoy.

McCoy pulled up a chair. "If this meeting brings up any questions, I figured it would be handy to have Miss Prescott right here."

Chief Gallagher was the next to show up in his neat blue uniform. "Looks like I'm not the last to arrive, I like that," he exclaimed.

Deputy Waldecker was a full fifteen minutes behind everybody else. "Sorry I'm late," he said. "But I had a little business up by your subject's house this morning."

"What happened?" asked Michael.

"I'm not really sure that anything happened. We got

a call that the State boys had tagged an abandoned vehicle and I had to go have a look and sign the tow order. It was actually right in front of Brian Prescott's property. A pickup truck owned by a local businessman pulled off the road and parked in the weeds down in the ditch. It's not a deep ditch, just kind of a low spot off the shoulder of the road. The truck was driven down there, not some out of control thing. We're trying to get in touch with the owner right now but no luck so far."

Chief Gallagher chimed in, "Pretty desolate stretch of road right there. Can't think of any reason anybody would be out that way unless they were poaching or something. Whose truck is it?"

Deputy Waldecker checked his notes. "Says here, Stanley Walchak"

"Driller," replied Chief Gallagher.

"I know who he is," said Michael, "Short guy. Owns a well drilling company?"

"Right," proclaimed the chief, "Probably not for much longer though. He inherited the place from his father a few years back and he's been running the business into the ground ever since. No pun intended."

McCoy and Bonnie Prescott had been silently sitting and listening to the conversation and finally McCoy loudly cleared his throat.

A blushing Michael quickly apologized and made the introductions around the table. He explained who Bonnie was and suggested that, since she was the client it would be appropriate to bring her up to speed on what they'd learned so far and what their future plans were.

When they were finished Bonnie spoke. "I wouldn't

bother using the taxpayer's airplane. I'll charter whatever you need for as long and as often you might need it and that goes for boats as well. I want this investigation to move along as quickly as possible. I won't get in your way but you will have my full support for anything you might need. All I ask is that you update me whenever you uncover anything new."

Michael leaned forward. "Miss Prescott, we couldn't possibly ask for anything more. Thank you." McCoy nodded in agreement.

Bonnie excused herself and left without ordering breakfast.

"Man," said the police chief, "That's the kind of client I'd want if I was a P.I."

"Me too," echoed the deputy.

"Okay. Let's get started," said Michael, "Can either one of you connect me with a reliable charter pilot who can handle what we want to do? And how about a big wide, stable boat?"

McCoy added, "And while you're at it, you know any shark experts?" Everyone began to laugh but then Deputy Waldecker said, "Actually one of our local Department of Natural Resources officers is an Elasmobranchologist."

"A what?" asked McCoy.

"They're scientists who study sharks. Officer Dee Phelps is a local gal who was planning a career in the shark business down in Florida when her mother was diagnosed with MS and she moved back here to care for her. Since she had a degree in marine biology, the DNR gobbled her up. They didn't have any research positions open at the time so they offered her a job in enforcement, you know a game warden. She liked it and stayed on. The lady sure knows her sharks though."

When Michael and McCoy walked out of the restaurant, they were armed with the names and phone numbers of a handful of charter boat captains, two of whom were part-time fishing charter captains and full-time cops. Deputy Waldecker said he'd handle the air surveillance chores. They had the phone number of the local Elasmobranchologist too.

CHAPTER 17

Brian was unsure of just what was happening. He found plenty of evidence that Shorty had somehow fallen into the shark pen and they had attacked him. It was an accident and nobody could blame Brian. He only wished that he could have been there to witness it. But then, the following afternoon when he was on his way home he pulled into a McDonald's to pick up a coffee and he was almost certain that he saw Shorty run out the back door and hightail it down a side street. He was tempted to follow but he wanted to keep a low profile. Besides, it was clear that Shorty was dead. But now as he watched the towing company haul the pickup truck out of the ditch right next to his driveway he wasn't so sure. Could Shorty have discovered the shark pen and used it to settle one of his own scores? That would explain the presence of a strange pickup truck as well as the phantom sighting yesterday. He decided to check out the crew shack that Shorty had been staying in.

As Brian looked around, he tried to focus on what wasn't there rather than what was there. There was no money lying around and no spare cigarettes. Shorty always had a few packs stashed away. He seemed to remember Shorty having a jacket and that was gone too. There were plenty of signs of a planned escape. Now Brian regretted not at least leisurely cruising the neighborhood streets around the McDonald's yesterday.

If Shorty had indeed used the sharks to kill someone, it would be somewhat less of a problem but still a problem. For now, he would have to assume that if Shorty was alive, he was on the run from the cops as well as from Brian. In the short term that would have to be good enough but it would need to be addressed before it became a headache. And Brian was having enough serious headaches as it was. The kind of headaches that were brought on by the voices screaming mercilessly in his head. Time was becoming a factor too. The big summer festival would begin in less than a week and that's when Brian's plan would see its hour of glory. He couldn't let anything stand in the way.

He had dreamed of causing panic and terror for years and now it was so close. When the thoughts of creating mass chaos first came to him he fought them. His parents had raised him to respect human life and he knew that his fantasies were wrong… totally wrong. Yet something, maybe the screaming voices possessed him and drove him to plan. Inheriting his grandparents' home and all that it included was probably what had pushed him over the edge. It was just too perfect. He had visualized the scenario over and over. The beach at the county park would be overflowing during the summer festival. Brian had visited the beach many times, often dining on one of those delicious deli corned beef sandwiches that they served at the beach restaurant. Sometimes he showed up looking like a tourist with a beach blanket and portable radio and on other occasions he dressed like a local. The beach was always a busy place during the summer and the traffic would multiply a hundredfold during the festival. There would be beach volleyball, concerts, and sand castle building contests. The festival lasted over a week so there would surely be at least a few blistering hot days that would bring over a thousand people to the beach. When the time was right, he would use his grandfather's fishing tug to tow the large cage containing nine hungry sharks and he would open the gate on the cage as soon as he was close to the bathing beach. Bull sharks had an extra keen sense for detecting prey at quite a distance and there would undoubtedly be hundreds of swimmers churning up the nearby waters. He would be starving the sharks for about three days ahead of time to make sure that they were extra hungry.

Getting away after releasing the sharks would present its own challenges but Brian had a plan for that too. The modifications that he'd made on the fishing trawler would allow him to totally change its appearance in less than a few hours. If his plan created the right amount of havoc, he'd have plenty of time to make the transformation.

He was almost ready to hire a couple of helpers for the final phase of the plan. All that was left was the construction of the cage that he'd tow behind the trawler and the installation of the false superstructure on the boat. Brian was particularly proud of the camouflage that he'd come up with. He had bought an old, wooden, rotting cabin cruiser on the other side of the state and had hauled it back here last fall. He planned to carefully remove everything above the main deck, including the old flying bridge. A few cans of spray paint and it would look as good as new; at least from a distance. It was basically nothing more than the roof and part of the deck of the main cabin with all of the windows intact. According to his measurements it would fit over the top of the sparse outline of the fishing trawler if he simply removed the shack-like cabin that served as the trawler's pilot house. Adding a few downriggers, fishing rod holders, and a couple of antennas would make it look enough like any one of the scores of charter boats that populated every marina on the bay. On the chance that somebody saw a cruiser releasing the sharks, investigators would be looking for an entirely different kind of boat.

CHAPTER 18

Department of Natural Resources officer Dee Phelps was dressed a lot more like a farm girl than a marine biologist. Today she was wearing Bermuda shorts, a sleeveless gingham blouse, and Nike's. She was rather short, maybe five two but built like a tennis player. She didn't carry any extra weight but she certainly had well-defined muscles. Her deep suntan, fresh-looking face, big brown eyes, and shoulder-length curly auburn hair gave her that wholesome country look. She was enjoying her day off at a quiet little place called 'The Farmer's Bar,' naturally, in the heart of farm country. She was drinking a beer and shooting pool with a couple of local farmers who were killing a little of the slack time between planting and harvest. The two men who had just wandered in the door were strangers to her but their demeanor was familiar, they had to be cops. She didn't acknowledge their presence but she could certainly feel the sweep of their eyes as they moved to a booth near the back door. It probably wasn't a coincidence that the only other table in the bar that had any drinks sitting on it was right next to that booth. The men ordered beer, a pitcher and two glasses.

Officer Phelps finished sinking the six ball and whiffed on the four. She strolled across the room to the table to grab a swig of beer.

"Are you the DNR officer?" asked Michael O'Conner quietly.

Phelps studied him for a moment before softly replying, "Off-duty at the moment. Should I know you?"

Michael was thankful for the opening. "We're private investigators looking into the welfare of the relative of our client and we've come across some unusual circumstances. We were hoping you'd be willing to help us out."

"Unusual how?"

"It has to do with sharks." Michael almost whispered.

Officer Phelps immediately picked up on Michael's discreet tone and said "You must be the guys Deputy Waldecker told me about. I'll be through here in a minute and then we can talk."

Phelps made short work of the pool game, running the table before saying to the other players, "I gotta go reminisce with a couple of old work buddies. Catch you later."

"No problem Dee, we have to run anyway." The farmers put up their cues and headed for the parking lot and their dusty pickup trucks.

Officer Phelps pulled up a chair next to the booth and asked. "Okay, what's this about sharks?"

McCoy glanced over at the bar and saw that the bartender was busy talking on a cell phone but just the same he got up and fed the juke box a dollar in exchange for a little cover noise.

Officer Phelps smiled. "You don't have to worry about him." She tilted her head toward the bartender. "He's one of the few I really trust around here, retired investigative reporter for a major newspaper in Cleveland. He covered the crime beat and loves digging in. He was born and raised less than a mile from here. It helps that he spent thirty years dealing with cops. Knows when to keep quiet, one of my best resources."

McCoy nodded and began. "What we'd like to know about is bull sharks."

"I thought you were looking into someone's welfare." Phelps had a puzzled look on her face.

"Well it's a little complicated but the object of our investigation is a rather reclusive guy and his sister is worried that he's up to no good. He's got a history of anti-social behavior."

"Any arrests?" asked Phelps.

"No," answered McCoy, "but he's a shark nut, specifically bull sharks and that's what we're concerned about."

"That's what *he's* concerned about," said O'Conner pointing to detective McCoy.

Phelps smiled. "Okay then. How can I help?"

"First of all, could bull sharks survive in the water around here?" asked McCoy.

"The short answer would be yes and no." Phelps moved in a little closer. "They have no problem adapting to fresh water and there is plenty for them to eat. The big fish like the King Salmon and Lake Trout would easily fatten them up."

"Where does the 'no' come in?" asked McCoy.

Phelps took a tug on her beer and said, "The studies aren't really complete on this but I doubt that they could handle the winters. They're not known to be found in lakes that freeze."

Michael began jotting down notes. "But they'd be fine in the summer?"

"Absolutely," responded Phelps.

"Aggressive?" chimed in Michael.

"All predators are aggressive when they're hungry and bull sharks are always hungry. Oh, and their bodies are about eighty-five percent muscle. To put that in perspective, humans are around twenty percent," answered Officer Phelps.

"I guess you've told us as much as we need to know," said McCoy. "Can we contact you if we have any new questions?"

"Sure, I'd be glad to help. If you actually do have any sharks around here, I'm sure I'll be right in the middle of it anyway. Let's exchange phone numbers. I'm thinking that we might want to sit down with Deputy Waldecker and the four of us can brainstorm this thing."

CHAPTER 19

Shorty made a lot of progress during his nighttime walk. Fear had caused him to quicken his pace considerably. Dawn was breaking now and he was hidden in the thick 10-foot-tall rushes along the swampy banks of the Quanicassee River. There wasn't much solid ground in the area but he had been able to follow a wild game path to a pleasant little clearing a couple hundred feet from the highway. Humans simply wouldn't have any reason to come back here. At least there were no signs that anybody frequented the spot. His tent was set up and the sleeping bag waited for him inside. Time for a little nourishment and a reflective moment with a cigarette before he tried for some dreamless sleep. He was tired of walking, tired of contending with all of the insects, and tired of being afraid.

Driller had never been his friend but he wouldn't have wished that kind of fate on anybody. He wondered if Driller had a family. He wondered if Driller's death would ever even be reported. The things that he heard Brian ranting about back in that boat house didn't make a bit of sense. Why would he have said things like, "I would have let you live a *little* longer?" What was with the sharks? It certainly wasn't like an aquarium or anything. Those were man-eating fish and could have only been put there for some evil purpose. Shorty wasn't real smart and he knew it so he often took it for granted that other people knew what they were doing. But this situation had him deeply puzzled and deeply worried. Perhaps if he slept on it things would become clearer. He crawled into his tent and zipped the door shut. He didn't need any snakes or muskrats seeking refuge in his little home. It was a warm day and Shorty slept fitfully on top of his sleeping bag, his jacket rolled up and serving as a pillow. The built-up fatigue brought on by adrenaline and a fourteen-mile walk on out-of-condition legs allowed him to sleep off and on for almost nine hours.

Now he was sitting on a stump boiling some water on his Sterno camp stove so that he could have a cup of instant coffee. He would have really preferred a cold beer, couldn't remember the last time he'd gone over twenty-four hours without one. Too much daylight left for him to risk taking to the highway so he decided to use the time piecing together the events of the last couple of days and figure out what to do about it. His conscience was giving him a hard time. Even though he never liked Driller, he felt compelled to do something about his terrible death. Going to the sheriff seemed like the logical thing but the bad blood between him and Driller was no secret around town and there had been no witnesses when Driller accidentally fell into the water. He would surely become a murder suspect and he had no money for lawyers. The thought of going to jail horrified him. But something had to be done. That Brian guy was dangerous and who knows what he might be up to next.

In a few hours it would be dark enough to resume walking. By his calculations he was less than ten miles from the mobile home park where his wife waited and figured that he could be there by dawn tomorrow even on his aching legs. With his face buried in his hands Shorty remained seated on the stump for more than an hour, confused about his future, confused about his direction, and confused about things in his recent past. It all seemed too horrible to be true. Had he been dreaming? When he finally looked up the sun was gone from the sky. Time to break camp and get back on the road. As he slung the backpack into place and adjusted the shoulder straps the fear crept into his mind once again.

She held the seemingly ancient dried flower in her hand, turning it over and over remembering every petal. It was the only thing left from the sparse and humble wedding day that she shared with Shorty some fifteen-odd years ago. She couldn't even recall who the witnesses were. They had been acquaintances of the magistrate who performed the ceremony. Shorty and Sharon were originally attracted to each other because of a common need. Neither was sophisticated, neither was considered good-looking, and neither had ever experienced any success in the dating scene. Two ugly misfits drawn to each other by their mutual repulsiveness. But Sharon didn't see it that way. Shorty may have been the butt of legions of jokes and he certainly must have been bullied throughout his adolescent years but to Sharon he was everything. She chose not to see any of his flaws and he never seemed to notice any of hers, a match made in heaven.

Now she was worried. Shorty had called yesterday and sounded panicked. He was talking so fast she couldn't understand most of what he was saying and then he just disappeared. She had heard nothing since. She remembered that he sounded more terrified than she'd ever heard him. It had scared her and now… nothing. All she knew was that he was somewhere between Bay City and Caseville and he sounded like he was running for his life. Then she thought about the conversation that she'd had with that young private detective. Maybe he knew something. She frantically dug through her purse looking for his card.

CHAPTER 20

As he sat in the booth in the little out-of-the-way restaurant waiting for McCoy to show up for lunch, Michael O'Conner was trying to research the habits of bull sharks. His concentration on the computer screen was interrupted by the ringing of his cell phone. The call was coming from an unfamiliar phone number.

"O'Conner Investigations."

"Hello, this is Sharon Stueber, the lady you talked to in Bay City a couple of days ago."

"Oh, hi," answered Michael, "Have you heard from your husband? Did he tell you where he is?"

"That's why I'm calling." Her voice sounded distressed. "He called home yesterday and he starts jabbering so fast I can't understand what he was saying and then all of a sudden he stops talking. Then the phone goes dead as if somebody hung it up. I know something terrible has happened, I just know it."

"Have you called the police?"

There was a hesitation and then Sharon replied, "Shorty don't like calling the police, don't trust them. He never wants the cops involved. Besides, I wouldn't even know which police department to call, I don't have no idea where he is."

"Mrs. Stueber, I'm afraid I can't help you. I have no authority or resources to investigate anybody's disappearance under suspicious circumstances. You'll have to start with your local police department and go from there."

"Isn't there anything you can do?" she pleaded.

"I wish there was but my license only allows me to investigate suspected criminal cases if the police approve it. I'll be glad to tell the police everything that I know and see if they'll authorize me to proceed but that's about all I can offer. And it might not even be relevant. But if he calls you again, give him my number and tell him to contact me. Maybe I could help if I knew just what his problem is."

Sharon Stueber began to sob on the other end of the line. "I just don't know what to do. Am I the only one in the world who cares about Shorty?"

Michael didn't answer the question but he thought, *you might just be right.*

"Call your local police department right now and give them my phone number. Tell them to contact me for more information. It's the best I can do."

Sharon agreed and signed off.

McCoy was standing next to the table when Michael looked up. "Did you hear any of that?" asked Michael.

"Only the part about you doing the best you can do. Why? What's up?" McCoy slid into the booth opposite Michael.

"It's kind of a long story," Michael began, "but do you remember me telling you about that guy from Bay City that I think might have hooked up with our boy Brian?"

"That 'Shorty' guy? Yeah, you've mentioned him.

Thought he might have gone to work for Brian on one of his boats or something."

"Right, well, I don't know anything for sure. It's just a guess at this point. That was his wife on the phone. Seems like he called her yesterday all frantic about something. She couldn't make any sense out of what he was saying and then the call disconnected. She thinks somebody's chasing him and she thinks that that somebody might be Brian."

McCoy rubbed his forehead. "Sounds like a police problem at this point."

"That's what I told her," said Michael, "They're one of those families who don't trust the cops. She didn't want to call them."

McCoy shook his head. "Under those circumstances we can't get involved unless it's calling the cops ourselves."

"Yeah, I know. I told her that she could give my number to the police and I'd tell them everything I know."

McCoy smiled. "And everything you suspect."

Michael nodded. "Yeah, right. Everything I suspect. This whole case is a hundred percent suspicion and speculation. We don't have one shred of evidence that anyone has done anything wrong or that anyone is actually missing."

McCoy signaled the waitress that he wanted to order. She smiled and headed over to the booth.

Michael looked up from his laptop, "Anything new on the owner of that truck they hauled out of Brian's ditch?"

"Not much," answered McCoy, "They're still trying to find him. He didn't show up for work this morning and that's unusual because he's the boss. Still nothing that would give the Sheriff cause to search the property."

Brian Prescott made it a point to visit Miller's Bar down in Bay City the last two nights. He didn't talk to anybody in the bar, he just watched and waited. The Durango sat out of sight on a side street over a block away. It felt like time wasted and unnecessary risk, besides he didn't like the way the bartender kept eyeing him. He wasn't completely sure if it was Shorty who had fallen victim to the sharks or whether it was Shorty's way of settling a score with an enemy. But the little guy didn't seem smart enough to handle the elaborate planning that would be required. The odds pointed to Shorty as being the shark victim. Gut feelings were notoriously unreliable and often led to a waste of time. Brian decided that he wouldn't be hanging around in this place tomorrow night. He had more important things to do. The summer festival was a little less than a week away. He needed to get the cage ready and that meant hiring a couple of helpers. His plan was to pick up a couple of indigents. The town was crawling with them. He'd avoid the homegrown ones with local relatives and community ties. He'd seek out the drifters, unemployed construction types. Preferably a couple of guys who were pretty new in town and without driver's licenses. He'd been scouting the local taverns for weeks and had his eye on two that looked like they would fit his plan perfectly.

CHAPTER 21

Michael O'Conner, McCoy, and Deputy Waldecker circled high above the Charity Islands in Saginaw Bay as they discussed their strategy. The Cessna 182 wasn't the county airplane, it belonged to a flying club in the area. The investigators didn't want to fly over Brian Prescott's complex in an aircraft with *Sheriff's Department* painted in big letters on the fuselage.

Michael was busy fitting the powerful telephoto lens to his digital camera while McCoy and Waldecker went over the charts.

"I don't want it to look like a surveillance flight so we won't be able to make more than one or two passes at low level," said Waldecker. "We'll have a quick peek from about 1000 feet up and then take a closer look. It's a procedure that we use all the time when we're ferreting out marijuana patches. They never catch on."

McCoy chimed in, "But this Brian guy might just be a little sharper than your typical weed farmer."

"Could be," replied Waldecker, "but if he's not expecting us and if we can catch him doing anything suspicious, we'll have reasonable cause for a personal visit. Ready to begin the mission?"

From where O'Conner was sitting he could clearly make out the coastline from Caseville to Sand Point and beyond into Wildfowl Bay. The water went from a deep blue over the open waters of Saginaw Bay changing to green and becoming lighter as it approached the point that jutted over five miles out from the mainland and then resolving to dark and foreboding as it swept around the peninsula into the murky bottom of the wetlands. A few inhospitable-looking islands dotted the area known as Wildfowl Bay. Brian Prescott's property stood out from the swampy-looking landscape, its neatly tended grounds, bright green lawn, and stately-looking house shined in stark contrast to the unfriendly appearance of the surrounding terrain. The docks looked uncluttered with two vessels moored at opposite ends. One was obviously a fishing tug and the other looked more like a barge with some heavy construction machinery resting on its deck. There appeared to be a large boathouse at the south end of the dock whose entrance was partially blocked by the thousands of cattails that thrived in the area. There was some kind of smaller building at the north. A large cabin cruiser sat in a cradle on dry land near the dock and there was some sort of commercial truck parked under a tree nearby. The place seemed to be shielded from the open water by a 200 foot barrier of cattails. Channels at either end of the dock were cut through the vegetation and gave the boats access to the bay beyond.

"How deep would you say is the water at the dock?" asked Michael.

Waldecker answered right away. "My best guess would be somewhere between 8 and 10 feet in the dredged channels although some of them are as deep as sixteen. Wildfowl Bay only goes about twenty to thirty-five. There's no deep water until you're out into the Saginaw Bay portion and then it doesn't get much over 50 feet until you're into the shipping channel and then it drops off to about seventy or so."

Michael had his camera clicking away as long as the place was still in sight while McCoy manned the video camera. The plane flew at minimum speed over their target so that there was plenty of opportunity to take pictures. McCoy leaned over the seat. "You should have a pretty good variety by the time we're done here." Michael nodded.

The plane made a wide sweeping turn and dropped its altitude to what felt like treetop level to O'Conner and McCoy. "I'll need a quicker trigger finger at this height," remarked O'Conner. He strained against his seatbelt to get closer to the window.

Waldecker made a slow pass in front of the house about 100 feet out over the water and then circled around behind the buildings to get a different perspective. "That's about all we'll be able to get," he said as he took the plane back over the farm country before climbing to an acceptable altitude. "Going through all those pictures should give you something to do this afternoon."

After the plane landed at the Huron County Airport, the three men gathered at a small coffee shop for a quick debriefing.

"I didn't see anything that would give me cause to enter the property on official business," mused the deputy.

"Yeah, I was thinking the same thing," chimed in McCoy, "Hopefully we'll be able to pick out some better detail when we go through the pictures."

Deputy Waldecker got up and shook hands with his

two new friends and said,"Gotta run now. Let me know if you see anything that warrants a closer look. And if you're still interested in doing a water approach, I can help with that too."

Back in his hotel room Michael sorted through the photos. Nothing seemed very suspicious-looking. The house and the outbuildings looked innocent enough. The boats seemed to belong there. There was what looked like an older cabin cruiser sitting up in a cradle near the dock with ladders leaning against either side as if somebody was working on it. Parked under a broad oak tree was some sort of a fairly large truck, just the nose sticking out. It wasn't a new vehicle but it didn't look very old either. None of the photos had a good enough angle to see the whole truck. It was a pretty husky-looking rig though and Michael wished that he could see the whole thing. It could be significant.

He observed very rugged-looking coastline that eventually melted into a peaceful homestead and then continued southward abruptly returning to an untamed environment. He stared at the series of pictures wondering why they didn't look quite right.

Finally he saw it. Symmetry. That's what was missing. The scene was out of balance. Coming from the north there was a gradual transition in the landscape but the southern edge suddenly turned from friendly to hostile as if there had been an imaginary dividing line. And that line seemed to purposely isolate the boathouse from the rest of the neatly manicured scene. He zoomed in on the south end of the dock for a closer look. There was a straight line there all right and it wasn't imaginary. Michael concentrated on the area and slowly a geometric pattern emerged from the maze of cattails. He traced the faint line through the tangled marsh reeds. Judging from the surroundings, he estimated that it was a rectangular shape about 30 feet on each side and just about the exact width of the channel. There was a line of old wooden pilings running east and west through the tall marsh grass that looked like it might have been the southern end of the fishing dock in bygone days. If that man-made looking section could be pulled out of the photo, the landscape would fall into balance. It had to be artificial, a floating island of cattails. But why? Is something hidden underneath?

Michael printed out the sequence of pictures and then highlighted the area in question. It was even more obvious on paper. A million scenarios raced through Michael's mind. The floating island, if that's what it was, had to be constructed to hide something. And whatever that something was would be hidden under water. He tried to block the image of sharks from his mind. It was way too far fetched. It couldn't be sharks. It just couldn't.

CHAPTER 22

He was no closer to a resolution or a plan of action than he had been when he first fled from the boathouse. Maybe the answer would come when he got home and had a chance to talk with his wife. Maybe not.

It'll be a lot easier walking as the night wears on, reasoned Shorty as he trudged along the side of the road. Too many cars in the early part of the evening, he thought. He was only able to walk short distances and then he'd have to hunker down so that passing cars wouldn't see him. In some areas he was able to get a ways off the road and made much better time but there were farmer's fences to contend with and stumps to trip over. It was rough walking no matter how he did it.

It was pretty much all farm country now and eventually he began seeing the recognizable landmarks that seemed to spring up out of the fields, a greenhouse, a fruit stand, a bar. The front door of the tavern stood open in the summer warmth and the juke box sounds mixed with laughter floated across the road to Shorty's ears. God, he wanted a beer but he was far too afraid to take the chance. He pushed on occasionally glancing back over his shoulder until the bar was far behind him. He had no idea what time it was but traffic was beginning to slow so he figured it must be somewhere around midnight. He guessed that he was within four miles or so of home. In the distance he heard a car coming up behind him and so he drifted farther from the road and flattened himself against the ground about four rows into a cornfield. He could tell by the change in the pitch of the engine that the car was slowing down. The singing sound that the tires made told him that they were coarse tread, off-road tires like you'd find on an SUV or a four-wheel drive pickup truck.

The vehicle continued to slow until it was just creeping along the road. Looking back, Shorty saw a powerful flashlight come on and begin sweeping its way back and forth across the cornfield. He was suddenly glad that his new backpack was made of a camo cloth. He shivered when he thought back to when he bought it and remembered that the first one he looked at had been bright red. He was terrified. He must have waited too long to jump for cover and been seen. Now he'd be in for a horrible death. The tires were making a crunching sound now.

The car had moved to the shoulder of the road and Shorty could see the flashlight beam creeping closer and closer to where he was hiding. He was wearing brown work pants and his body was mostly concealed by the furrow that ran parallel to the road. Maybe that would be enough to save him. The shaft of light came closer and closer. Shorty swore he could feel the heat of the beam as it crossed his body from foot to head. But it didn't stop, didn't even slow down. The car crept along the highway for another hundred yards or so and then the flashlight suddenly went black and the car accelerated back on to the road. In minutes the taillights were just dim devil eyes flickering on the horizon.

When Shorty finally pulled his quivering body to

an upright position, he was wringing wet with nervous perspiration. He reasoned that it could have been just a poacher who thought that he'd seen a deer cross the road. After all, the area was full of people who preferred living off the land to visiting a butcher shop. Shorty knew dozens of families who lived on wild game. But he didn't believe the logic. In his current state of mind every sound, every whisper of breeze represented a madman who would be charging out of the darkness at any moment with a razor-sharp machete whistling through the air. To say he was a nervous wreck would be an understatement.

He was getting close to town and automobile traffic was beginning to increase significantly. When he finally reached the residential area he found himself navigating his way through the winding, circular streets of the trendy subdivisions that surrounded the old city. It wasn't as scary here but it was frustratingly slow, and frustratingly confusing. He escaped the last tangled layout of meandering concrete and found himself in a weedy field that was no more than three hundred yards from the mobile home park where he lived. The only problem was that it was all open country between him and his sanctuary and the sun was rising rapidly in the east. The cover of darkness was lost. He stood in the shadow of the hedges that surrounded the subdivision he'd just emerged from and he surveyed the scene. With the housing development at his back and the mobile home park directly in front of him, he was protected from two sides but totally exposed on the other two. He was just about in the center between two roads less than a half mile apart that both carried heavy rush hour traffic. He began to shake again, his refuge was in plain sight, straight ahead but lethal danger lurked to his right and to his left.

He talked himself into calming down enough to think and to plan. He slowly lowered his body to the ground and stretched out on his stomach. Safety was only the length of a couple of football fields away. He had to make it. Grabbing handfuls of the tall grass he began pulling himself slowly across the field on his belly like a soldier in enemy territory.

Sharon Stueber hadn't slept much last night. Today was a rare day off from both of her jobs but tomorrow would be a full shift. The tears continued to flow as she plugged in the coffee maker. She didn't know what to do. Shorty sounded scared when he called but he never mentioned calling the police. She didn't want to make him mad but on the other hand she needed to make sure he was safe. She finally decided to wait until ten o'clock. If there was no word by then she'd have to go to the cops.

She heard the door rattle and pulled back the curtain on the kitchen window. By leaning across the sink and craning her neck she could just barely see the front porch. All she could make out from this angle was a backpack and some legs. But the legs looked familiar. She ran to the door and saw Shorty, hair a tangled mess, three days' worth of scraggly beard stubble and his eyes bulging as big as saucers frantically looking around him as he shook the doorknob. It took a few seconds for Sharon to calm Shorty down enough to let go of the doorknob so that she could unlock it.

Arms flailing, he burst through the door, slammed it behind him and immediately locked it. "I've been running all night. Make sure everything is locked and all the drapes are closed," he shouted as he ran through the double-wide going from window to window cranking them all tightly closed and flipping the locks. Sharon followed, pleading with him to stop and tell her what was going on. But Shorty was too panicked to hear her. He kept running around checking and rechecking, only stopping once in a while to open the drapes an inch or so to scan the surrounding landscape.

Sharon caught up to him and began tugging at the backpack. "What's with this thing?" she asked.

Shorty stopped momentarily and wiggled out of the harness. "I needed it," he gasped, "had to sleep in the woods and stuff. I couldn't let him find me."

"Who? What are you talking about? You're home safe now. Catch your breath and tell me."

Shorty stopped, stood motionless in front of her and then fell onto the couch crying uncontrollably. Sharon ran to him and cradled him in her arms as a mother would her baby. She stroked his wet hair and kissed his sweaty forehead. Gradually the tears subsided and he just sobbed. He didn't say a word as his chest continued to heave. His breathing continued to slow until it was almost normal and finally it settled into a deep steady rhythm.

Sharon gently placed a pillow under his head and found a light sheet in the linen closet to cover him. She picked up the backpack that Shorty had dropped on the floor and deposited it in a chair next to the door. She would love to know what was inside of it but she'd never think of invading Shorty's privacy. He'd more than likely show her everything when his sanity returned. She was sure that a good long nap would help bring him back. He said that he'd been running all night and sleep deprivation combined with the stress that fear brings can do horrible things to your mind. Sleep was like a reset button. All the same she made it a habit to spend the next six hours going from window to window, discreetly peeking out to see if anything unusual would catch her eye. All was quiet. Whatever Shorty was running from was surely frightening, real or imagined.

CHAPTER 23

It had taken a lot of work and careful study for Brian to identify the men he wanted. All of the locals, no matter how reclusive or isolated, had to be avoided. Small towns seemed to know everybody's business even if they had no business at all. The men he needed had to be drifters, social misfits with absolutely no local ties. He had found two of them, both in their mid to late fifties and both wondering where their next meal was coming from. Brian had nicknamed them "Flim" and "Flam" in his mind. They had arrived in town as part of a crew that was installing cable television lines but had lost their jobs by missing too much time on drunken binges. Now they found themselves stranded. This afternoon he discovered them sitting on the breakwall that guarded the harbor just outside of town, sharing one can of beer and using a stick for a fishing rod with a few feet of monofilament line trying to catch dinner, hopefully a walleye or a perch or two.

"Are they biting?"

The taller man looked up, his eyes grateful that they weren't looking at a game warden. "Nothing yet but we've only been here an hour or so."

"I don't know if you remember me but we talked a week or so back about a possible job."

The man studied Brian for a moment before replying.

"Yeah, I remember you. Seems like you had some sort of a building project, assembling some kind of prefab something. Was it a garage?"

"Not a garage but it's something about that size. Are you guys available?"

The man with the fishing pole turned. "What's it pay? Will it be cash?"

Brian smiled at the man's cavalier attitude. The guy really had no choice. If the wage was only enough for one meal, he'd have to take it. He decided to toy with the men. "I was figuring somewhere in the neighborhood of twenty bucks an hour. And it would be straight cash."

Both men stood up but only one of them spoke. "It's gotta be either an awful dangerous job or something illegal. Nobody pays that kind of money around here."

"Neither," replied Brian, "It's just a job with a tight deadline. We're looking at twelve to fourteen hours of serious work and it's got to be done start-to-finish in one shot. I don't want any locals working on it and I don't want them to even know about it. The people I work for were quite insistent on that."

The two men looked at each other and nodded in unison. "We can be quiet," said one of them, "When do you want us to start?"

Brian peeled two twenties off of the roll in his pocket and handed one to each of the men. "Here's enough for a couple of hamburgers to get you through the night and I'll pick you up right here at six in the morning. Any questions?"

Both men shook their heads and Brian turned and marched off the seawall. When he got back to his place, he busied himself using the old propane-powered forklift to haul his materials from the storage shed out to the dock area. He placed three large bucketfuls of heavy-duty nylon wire ties on the dock. There were dozens of pallets of heavy netting and hundreds of feet of 1-inch diameter thick-wall black pipe as well as a barrel full of pipe fittings. A large tool cart sat at the edge of the work area, bristling with pipe wrenches, pry bars, and wire cutters. He worked all the way up until sunset getting the old motor barge into position and disconnecting the dredge bucket from the cable and replacing it with the big forged steel hook. Brian really liked the old barge. His grandfather had designed it for working in the tight channels that were slotted into the landscape throughout the eastern shoreline of Saginaw Bay. It was a one-of-a-kind self-propelled crane barge with a retrofitted five-ton crane, much smaller than the commercial versions but it suited his needs perfectly.

Brian was under duress the whole time he worked. He had been spooked a couple of days ago when an airplane had buzzed his property at low altitude. It didn't look like any kind of government plane and it didn't hang around very long. He knew that there were air charter services nearby who offered scenic rides along the waterfront and it was certainly the time of year for those flights but he'd never had one come so close in the past. They usually stayed out over the bay and circled the islands. All of his activities were well-covered and he was relatively certain that, even if it was some sort of government spy plane, there wasn't anything unusual to be seen from the air. Nonetheless, he feared a repeat visit and hoped that it wouldn't come tomorrow. There would be things going on that might just raise some eyebrows. Hopefully things would go smoothly and no one would be the wiser. The sharks hadn't been fed in a while and he was looking forward to watching them feast on Flim and Flam.

And then there was the matter of Shorty and the mysterious abandoned pickup truck that had been hauled away from a spot uncomfortably close to his property. The ideal scenario would be that the truck was simply an innocent breakdown and the owner had sent a wrecker to pick it up, and that Shorty had wandered into the boathouse on some curious notion and then somehow lost his balance and fallen into the shark pen. It was obvious that the sharks had attacked and devoured someone, they were still scavenging a few bits of flesh that could be seen floating on the surface when Brian discovered the scene. He only wished he'd been there to witness the slaughter.

The incident had given Brian the answer he needed to the question of how he could overpower two men and throw them into the shark pen. One of the walkways along the side of the pen was quite narrow and so the footing was less than sure. If he could get two people on that walkway and then somehow lever them into the water his problem would be solved. There had been an old utility pole lying up by the house for over a year. At one time it had supported a yard light but Brian did away with that the first week after he inherited the place. The pole was almost 50 feet long but Brian only needed about twenty or so. He sawed it in half and hauled a section down to the dock in front of the shark pen. There was an old hoist in the ceiling of the boathouse that was designed to lift a twenty-ton boat out of the water for winter storage or repair. Brian made up a spreader bar with four lifting lines attached. He fed the 20 foot section of utility pole through the loops in the lifting lines and then raised the hoist so that the pole hung about 2 feet above the water right over the center of the shark pen. Then he installed a series of brackets that supported a steel rail on the wall directly behind the narrow walkway. With the aid of a chain hoist, he was able to pull the four-hundred pound pole over to the wall of the boat hoist where he anchored it to the steel rail with a single point release mechanism. The release would be opened with an electrical solenoid triggered by any one of a number of push button switches mounted around the interior of the boathouse. When one of the buttons was pressed, it would release the catch and allow the pole to sweep from left to right across the walkway and across the shark pen like a giant trapeze bar. It was foolproof.

CHAPTER 24

Deputy Waldecker had requested the early evening meeting. His shift was over at 4:00 and he could be there by 6:00. Officer Dee Phelps was going to be there too. When McCoy and Michael walked in to the Farmer's Bar they were introduced to a man who said that he'd recently been inside the grounds of Brian Prescott's estate.

After handshake greetings all around Michael turned to Officer Phelps and said, "This must be your hangout, eh? Same place we met you last time."

"You can call it that if you want but I like the place because it's quiet and secure. After the first time we talked, I got ahold of Waldecker for more information and he kinda filled me in. Then I talked to Bob, the bartender here to see if he'd heard any rumblings about the old Prescott homestead and he put me on to Steve Kraus, the guy you just met. I've known Steve for years but didn't know about his connection with the old Prescott estate. Steve is the sole owner of a good-size trucking company and he says that he was at the Prescott place about a month ago."

"Great. Why don't we all sit down together and compare notes." Michael was pushing two tables together so they could get started.

McCoy pulled a notebook out of his shirt pocket and said, "Well Steve, what have you got for us?"

Steve Kraus was one of those guys that people immediately liked, easy going, an innocent-looking smile that charmed all the girls, and straightforward demeanor that compelled men to trust him. A young-looking fifty-year-old, his self-confidence would never be mistaken for arrogance. He rocked back in his chair.

"I've got a little trucking outfit a few miles from here, thirty tractors and about ninety assorted trailers. With all of those diesels I've got to make sure that I have mechanics on call at all times. I've got two full-time guys at the terminal and a pocketful of independent contractors on call. I need to be sure that someone is available at all times. I guess it was about two or three months ago that one of the part-timers called me up, saying that he got a call to take a look at an old diesel-powered crane barge over in Wildfowl Bay. He called me because I live over that way up on Sand Point and he had heard that all of those old companies in that area were out of business."

"But this isn't a fishery," interjected Michael.

"Doesn't matter," replied Steve, "There's nothing commercial in that neighborhood at all anymore. After the government declared it a wetland, none of the business permits could be renewed. They couldn't force people out of their homes but as businesses closed, the government bought up the property. It's been close to fifty years since they started and now the Feds own almost all of it. Anyway, my buddy was a little nervous about going out there alone because he'd heard stories about this Brian Prescott being a zombie or something like that."

Steve smiled and tipped the Bud Light bottle to his lips.

McCoy looked up from his notebook. "But why go to you? You've got to be a busy man, after all, you're the owner."

"In this part of the country you've got to be a hands-on guy if you want to be successful. I take my shift behind the wheel just like all the other drivers. Nobody sees me as being any different than any of the other drivers except I hand out the paychecks. I like that because I get to see smiles now and then." Steve laughed.

"So did you see anything that set off your radar when you were out there?" asked Michael.

"Nothing scary but it was interesting because it was like being in a time machine. First of all, there was this beautiful old house that sat on a little rise overlooking the bay. They used to build up the lots in that swampy area to keep the basements from flooding. It's a scene out of the early part of the last century. The grounds were neatly manicured and spotless. The only thing that looked out of place was an old mahogany Chris Craft Connie. Seemed to be about a 44 footer and it appeared as if someone was dismantling it. Out in front of the house is a really long, maybe 300 foot dock that's in excellent shape. At one end there was a little cabin, looked like a living quarters actually because it had a chimney and an electric meter. At the other end was a huge in-water boathouse that had big padlocks on all the doors. That struck me as strange because the little place on the other end of the dock didn't look like it had any kind of locks on the doors at all. Then there was an old fishing tug, a gill-netter, maybe a 48 or 50 footer tied up about midway on the dock and the old crane barge was moored down near the boathouse. It was the crane barge that Prescott had called about. He wanted some service done on the engine. As I understood it, the engine actually ran, it was just a little on the ragged side. Could've been anything from a clogged injector or a bad plug to a compression leak or bent valve. The engine hadn't been started in ages before Brian moved in and began tinkering with it so we were thinking that it was just some crud in the fuel. When we got there, this Prescott guy kept asking me who I was and why had I tagged along. I tried to be straight with him and told him that the mechanic just wanted someone knowledgeable to bounce ideas off of. But he was clearly nervous about me being there and hustled us out of there before we could even get near the old rig. Something was bothering him big-time."

"Hmmm," mused McCoy, "So you never got near that big secure boathouse, eh?"

"Not within a country mile," replied Steve.

Michael leaned forward. "Do you think it's possible to get a good look at the boathouse from out in the bay?"

Steve studied his Bud Light for a moment. "You'd probably be looking straight at the front door. Except that there's a lot of weeds and stuff blocking that channel right up near the boathouse. It's kind of strange too because the rest of the waterway is wide open. As I remember, it looked like it was lined up perfectly with the trench that led straight through all the cattails and emptied into the open water."

Michael looked at Deputy Waldecker. "Have you got access to a quiet boat that we could sneak in pretty close?"

"How about a sailboat?" chimed in Dee, "I've got a shoal draft 26 footer docked in Bay Port. It's a good boat for shallow waters and it's as quiet as the wind. There are sailboats all over that part of the bay all the time so it will be inconspicuous too. It's a real popular sailing area. Not many stink boats around there because they're too worried about clogging their water pickups with weeds. My boat is one of the older models with good-sized windows in the cabin. You can slide them open and stay back in the shadow and do all of your picture-taking from below decks. Nobody will see you in there."

"Sounds perfect," said Michael, "When can we do it?"

Waldecker jumped in, "The next time that both Dee and I have a free day is the day after tomorrow. And I understand that the weather will be ideal. Sunny with a light southwesterly breeze Will that work for anybody?"

"Things are looking up," said Michael, "looks like we've got a sailing party. What time?"

"No later than eight o'clock," said Dee.

"Is it okay if I tag along?" asked Steve.

"The more, the merrier," answered Dee.

CHAPTER 25

It was 5:30 in the morning when Brian pulled in near the big concrete pier that extended two hundred yards into Saginaw Bay. The sun was on its way into the sky over the lone fisherman who sat in a folding chair at the very end of the breakwall. A labrador retriever sat dutifully at his feet. It was looking like another beautiful summer day. He shut off the engine in his Durango and listened to an oldies station on the radio. He had been sitting there for around ten minutes when he heard voices approaching over his left shoulder. Turning slightly he could see Flim and Flam working their way up the path parallel to where he was parked. It looked like they were wearing the same clothes that they had on yesterday. He started the engine and tapped the horn. The two men waved and altered their course toward him. Brian jumped out and opened the back door. "Might as well hop in the back. More legroom back there. You guys had breakfast?"

Two heads shook in unison.

"Well, I've got some coffee and cinnamon rolls back at the house. That should get you started."

Flim replied, "That'll do just fine. By the way, I hope we aren't expected to bring our own tools. Everything we own is currently in a hock shop."

Brian looked back as he pulled out of the lot.

"No problem. I've got everything you need."

They rode in silence for the first part of the trip and then one of the men asked, "How far are we going? I thought you told us that this job was local."

"Only about two or three more miles and we'll be there," replied Brian. His answer seemed to satisfy them because nobody spoke until they turned into the driveway.

Flim again, "Wow, I never would have even seen this place, it ain't much more than a path."

"It doesn't get much traffic. I'm about the only one who uses it," said Brian. "I might get it paved one of these days."

When Brian slowed down to let the electronic gate slide open in front of them, the two men in the back seat looked at one another but neither of them spoke. The tree tunnel that they were driving through eventually broke into a picturesque clearing that hosted an elegant old house with a nice view of the bay. A quaint looking dock with a classic fishing boat bobbing gently next to the pilings completed the welcoming picture. "This is it," announced Brian.

The three men got out of the car and Brian led his two employees down to the dock. "I thought I'd explain the job and then we can run up to the house and attack those cinnamon rolls before we go to work." Flim and Flam nodded.

Brian gave the men a few instructions explaining that they would be building a portable live-well for transporting fish out into the bay. He told them that it was part of an experimental breeding program where they would be towing thousands of tagged fish to a spot at the northern end of the bay and then releasing them so that they could track their movements. The job today would be to construct the cage or container for the first batch.

"But why is it a secret?" asked one of the men.

"Because this isn't a government program," said Brian. "It's being handled by a private fish-and-game management group and they're in a competitive bidding war with a couple of other outfits. My boss is worried about corporate espionage."

Both men seemed satisfied with the answer and they all headed toward the big house for some sweet rolls.

An hour later all three of them were beginning to break a sweat. They started by building a large rectangular frame out of the heavy-duty pipe. Brian connected a chain sling to the first section and then started up the crane that sat on the barge. He hooked up the sling and then lifted the first section off the ground so that they could assemble and attach the next section. They repeated the process two more times and the end result looked like a somewhat square skeleton about 12 feet wide, 30 feet long and 8 feet high with most of one end open. Next they attached a large pipe gate to that opening. It was hinged on the bottom with a trip lever at the top so that, when the time came to open it, all that needed to happen was to pull on a rope. A latch would pop up and the gate would fall open. Brian tested it several times and it worked flawlessly.

"You guys have done a great job. We're ahead of schedule," Brian boasted, "Let's break for lunch."

They went up to the main house where Brian treated them to deep-fried chicken and cold beer. He went over the remaining tasks with his crew. The next step would be to "skin" the cage with some netting that he had prepared.

He'd use the forklift to stretch the sections of netting over the framework and they would wrap nylon wire-ties spaced at about six inches over the entire cage. The last step would be to attach the plastic barrels to the perimeter. Brian had done the calculations for just the right amount of cubic feet of flotation to maintain neutral buoyancy. Flim and Flam didn't question anything, they just nodded as they wolfed down almost 4 pounds of chicken.

Brian noted that both of his hired hands displayed experience and competence in their work. They seemed to get everything right on the first attempt and they worked well together. Progress was steady and by six in the afternoon they were ready for the immersion test. Brian climbed up on the crane barge, fired up the old diesel and lifted the cage. He coaxed the levers lightly and set the cage gently into the water, barely making a ripple. He kept lowering the hook until the cable went slack. The cage floated about twelve inches below the surface. Brian beamed with pride. Now he felt vindicated for weighing every inch of pipe, all of the fittings, every foot of reinforced netting, and even the nylon wire-ties. His calculations had been nothing short of perfect. He hauled the cage out of the channel and returned it to the grassy area behind the dock. He was pleased to see Flim and Flam returning all of the tools to the cart and picking up all of the scraps. It was obvious that they had been disciplined tradesmen at one time.

It was probably still a good two and a half hours until sundown and for Brian's plan to work he needed low light. He needed to stall the guys for a little while longer.

"You guys appreciate good rum?" he asked as he jumped from the barge.

"Ya mean the spiced kind?" asked Flim.

"Yep. You can have it straight up, with Coke, ginger ale, Sprite, you name it."

They both responded that they preferred ginger ale.

Brian invited them up to the house for the drink saying that they had done such a good job that he was going to keep them on the clock for a while longer. His employers had authorized a certain amount of money for construction of the cage and he still had some room under the cap. The men didn't argue. Drinking rum while you're getting paid? It doesn't get any better than that.

The shadows were getting long as the sun settled into the western bay. Brian had helped Flim and Flam with the Parrot Bay Rum, mixing his own special drink. The rum was beginning to make him lightheaded and so he stopped drinking and simply poured more for his guests.

Finally the blazing streaks of red and orange in the sky signaled the sunset and Brian decided to move. "You guys want to see what this thing is really all about?"

"Sure," said Flim. "I'm game," said Flam. "Follow me," said Brian.

Brian took a small LED flashlight from the holster on his belt and led the way down to the boathouse. Flim and Flam followed giggling like a couple of drunken teenagers.

"We've got a new species here, an eco-friendly strain of lake trout that were bred in South America. They're good for the environment as well as being a fierce battling game fish. They shouldn't force any other class of fish to compete for food since they're primarily a plankton feeder. Fine-tasting fish as well. They're gonna make the Great Lakes the number one destination for all sport fishermen." Brian unlocked the padlock and opened the door. It was almost dark inside the boathouse. The final remnants of daylight were halfheartedly pushing through the dusty windows. There was barely enough light to see the freshly painted white walkway. It was a scant 2 feet wide forcing them to walk single file. He walked in front of the two men as they inched their way up the narrow walk alongside the boat well. When they got about half way in, Brian stopped and said, "Stay right here, I'll go around the other side and turn on the lights." He turned and left Flim and Flam standing in the dark.

The two hired hands stood rigidly still facing the opposite wall of the boathouse. Brian was barely visible as he moved up the plank across from them, talking all the way.

"You guys did a good day's work for me today. I thought it would take almost twice as long. I appreciate your efforts. How does about $350 each sound for your time today?"

One of the men whistled and Brian heard them both say, "Sounds great." It didn't matter how much he promised them because Brian had no intention of allowing them to live long enough to collect it.

"Okay guys, prepare yourselves for the unveiling of a whole new generation of Great Lakes game fish." Brian momentarily flashed his ultra-bright LED flashlight at the men making sure that the beam hit them both directly in the eyes. Then he quickly turned on the bright overhead lights before their pupils could contract. As soon as he saw them both leaning forward trying to focus on the swirling water, he hit the button that released the giant log trapeze behind the men. The apparatus swung silently from its perch on the wall contacting the men just above the waist and flinging them like a couple of rag dolls into the center of the boat well. The sharks hadn't eaten for a couple of days and reacted immediately.

Brian, the voices shrieking inside his head, stood mesmerized by the sight of the boiling scene. Terror filled the eyes of the first man as his mind processed the meaning of the large dorsal fin that streaked in his direction. Brian watched as one shark grabbed the man by the legs while two others attacked his head and upper torso. The other man was able to flail his way to the dock where Brian stood but just as he reached for the piling, he was dragged back to the center of the fray where four more hungry sharks converged on his body. Brian thought that it was an amazing sight to watch the two men being thrown from one hungry mouth to the next. The power and efficiency of these fish was awesome. He was surprised at how long both men were able to remain conscious and screaming. It seemed like at least ten minutes although his mind told him that it was probably closer to three. The water slowly turned wine red as the hearts of the two men continued to pump. It seemed like the blood in the water served as an accelerant to the frenzy of the sharks. The havoc continued until the surface of the water was littered with tiny remnants of what had been two grown men. The sharks now circled slowly on the surface of the water cleaning up the last of the evidence. And then the boathouse was quiet once again.

Brian had always wondered what it would feel like to watch a man die in agony. Now he knew and it excited him beyond his wildest expectations. Staring into their pleading eyes as their bodies were being ripped apart gave him an unbelievable thrill.

He returned to the main house and uncapped the half full bottle of coconut rum. He poured a generous shot of the flavored rum into a water glass, added a couple more ingredients and christened his newly created cocktail "*The Nightmare.*" And then he hoisted a toast. "To Flim and Flam. I never knew your real names but henceforth you shall be known as Captain and Morgan." He swallowed the rum in one long drink and then crumpled into the big upholstered recliner to dream and celebrate his first two official murders. The screaming voices were gone. All was peaceful in Brian Prescott's world.

Out in the bay two teenage couples taking a moonlight cruise aboard a 28 foot sailboat turned down the boom box because one of the girls insisted that she heard someone screaming for help. The four of them stood quietly and listened for any sound. The girl who had first mentioned it was pointing eastward toward the weedy shore of Wildfowl Bay, "It came from over there." One of the boys chimed in, "I thought I heard it too only it sounded as if it was coming from that way." He was pointing due north about ninety degrees from the direction that the girl had indicated.

After what they considered a respectable amount of time spent straining their eyes at the barely visible shoreline, the teenagers decided that it might just have been a ghost signal coming in over the radio. They cranked up the volume of the FM station they were listening to and set their course for Bay Port.

CHAPTER 26

It had been almost seven hours since Shorty had staggered into the old double wide trailer that he called home. He woke up covered with sweat and reeking in the same clothes that he'd worn and slept in for the past four days. He sat up on the couch looking from side to side as if he was unsure of where he was. Sharon emerged from the back bedroom and quietly said, "You're home and you're safe. I've been keeping my eyes open and nobody has come looking for you. Believe me, you're safe."

Shorty stared at her for a moment and tears began to spill from his eyes. "Are the doors and windows all locked?"

Sharon nodded and tried to smile, "We need to get you cleaned up and get a good meal in you. I've got all the stuff to make tacos, it's your favorite. How's that sound?"

Shorty shrugged, dragged himself up from the couch and trudged into the bathroom where he found that Sharon had laid out clean underwear and clothes. He cried a little harder as he gently closed the door. As the hot water hammered on his back, Shorty finally began to feel as if he was in a safe place, at least for now. The shower helped to relax his tense muscles and for the first time in days he felt his heartbeat coming back to a more regular cadence. When he returned to the living area he found an ice-cold Budweiser sitting at his regular spot at the kitchen table. For the first time… he smiled.

Sharon knew Shorty well enough to know that he

would tell her everything as soon as he had it sorted out in his mind. She didn't push. She just smiled and served him his favorite meal. Shorty ate like an animal, barely coming up for air as he devoured taco after taco. When he was finally finished with his supper, he walked over and picked up his backpack, turned it upside down and emptied the contents on the couch. Sharon stood by his side. The largest item was a sleeping bag followed by a compact little sack that held a two-man tent. There were a few cans of Sterno-type fuel, a little camp stove and a Boy Scout-type mess kit. A handful of water bottles lay in a row next to a medium-sized sheath knife and one pack of Marlboros. There was also a small jar of instant coffee along with a half dozen energy bars, and three envelopes stenciled MRE. Sharon picked one of them up for a closer look.

"It stands for 'Meal Ready to Eat,'" said Shorty. "None of 'em are tacos though." They both chuckled.

Shorty sighed. "Well, here's what happened." He told Sharon about meeting Brian in Miller's Bar in Bay City and all about how they first started talking. He continued the tale covering his sudden hiring and the seemingly innocent work that he had done on Brian's fishing trawler. "I thought I had really impressed him," he added. He told her about his chance encounter and confrontation with Driller and the fact that there were dozens of witnesses to the shouting match. Then came the hard part. He got to the part about how his idle curiosity led him inside the 'off limits' boathouse and the discovery of the sharks. He began to choke up and sob when he had to relive the moment when Driller lost his balance and fell in with the man-eaters. "I didn't actually see him fall," he said. "I kinda heard it. But when I looked up I could see that they were attacking him from every direction. There was nothing I could do but watch. It all happened so fast. It was horrible."

Then he told her about Brian coming into the boathouse and how he went around stomping and yelling, totally out-of-control and what he said about letting someone live a while longer.

"That's what really scared me," said Shorty, "He didn't know anything about Driller. He thought it was me in there with the sharks and that's who he was talking to."

Sharon let out a long breath. "You must have been hidden pretty well or he would have seen you."

"He didn't have all of the lights turned on and I was back in the shadows. I don't think he really looked all that hard. After all he thought I was dead." Shorty shuddered as he said the words. "He finally went back into his house and after about a half hour he came back out, jumped in his car and left. That's when I made a break for it. I stayed out of sight during the day and I only walked at night. And then I'd hide every time I saw headlights coming. It was slow walking and for the first day I didn't have anything at all to eat. The only drink I had was from a faucet on the side of a gas station. It was bad that first day."

"When was it that you called? The second day?" asked Sharon.

"Yeah, I think so. I was so hungry that I took a chance and went into a McDonald's in broad daylight, I had just had a hamburger and fries and noticed that there was a pay phone on the wall. Almost as soon as you answered I saw that guy, that monster, pull into the lot. All I could think of was to run. He must not have seen me though because nobody chased me. That's when I found a sporting goods store and bought all of that camping gear. I knew that I'd be hiding in the woods during the daytime."

"Well, you're home now safe and sound and it looks like no one followed you here or we'd have known about it by now. Did you ever give your address to this Brian guy?"

Shorty thought for a minute. "Y'know he never asked about anything like that. He asked a couple of questions about my personal life but I never gave him no straight answers. He doesn't know that you even exist."

"I didn't want to worry you with this but I'd better let you know. There's been a private detective hanging around asking questions about a guy. He wanted me to find out the name of the man you were working for."

Shorty suddenly sat up straight. "How did he latch onto you? Where'd he come from? You didn't tell him nothing did you?"

"I had gone over to Miller's Bar to see if the bartender had any idea who you had left with on that first night. The private detective was standing there when I asked about you and he followed me outside. Honey, at that point I didn't know anything and I hadn't yet gotten that crazy phone call that scared me half to death. At the time it seemed pretty harmless. He gave me his card and said to get in touch with him if I needed anything. And then after that call you made from the McDonald's I talked to him again and said that I thought somebody was chasing you and wanted to harm you. I was worried out of my mind. How could I not have said anything? I asked him to help me find you."

Shorty had an anxious look on his face. "And?"

"He said he couldn't search for a person who was

missing under suspicious circumstances unless he had permission from the police. And until I filed a missing persons report he'd be powerless to help."

"So what did you tell him?"

"I said I'd call him back when I knew what I was gonna to do. Right now everything is in limbo. I hadn't made up my mind what to do and then you showed up."

Shorty seemed to relax slightly. "Well if he calls back tell him that everything is okay and it was all a big misunderstanding, that you didn't know what was going on and you overreacted. I don't want no cops involved, private or otherwise."

Sharon put her hand on Shorty's arm. "But what about that man who died, the one that the sharks killed?"

"It bothers the hell out of me too," replied Shorty, "But just the day before that I was in town playing Keno in a local bar and Driller starts yelling at me from all the way across the room. And I'm yelling back at him. Everybody in the whole place knows that there ain't no love lost between us. The next thing you know he's dead and there was only me and him in that boathouse. It'd sure look like I conned him into coming there and then pushed him in the water. I'd be charged with murder just as sure as you're standing there."

Sharon tapped her foot. "Yeah, I guess you're right. So what are we going to do?"

"All I can think of is to stay out of sight. If the cops catch up with that Brian guy, he sure as hell isn't gonna tell them about me. Right now I can't think of any way they can connect me with him or his place. I've gotta stay far away from Miller's Bar because that's where I met him. Other than that I don't know what to do."

CHAPTER 27

Once a year the small bay side city of Caseville hosts one of the largest and most successful events in the State of Michigan. With its beautiful waterfront location Caseville has always been a tourist destination, in the old days it was perch fishermen followed a few years later by bikers who were eventually replaced with hippies. Everyone came to enjoy the sugar sand beaches and the clear warm waters of the bay. The fishermen left trails of beer cans in their wake and the hippies trashed just about everything. Surprisingly the bikers pretty much cleaned up after themselves.

Some of the more forward-thinking business leaders in town saw the potential for some significant seasonal profits but what they needed was a unique theme, a way to draw hundreds of people to the quaint little town that boasts a downtown district a little over three blocks long and borders on a picturesque harbor. A large park with a major league bathing beach sits on the edge of town. Many of the merchants are snowbirds who close down their businesses from November through April and spend their winters in Florida. Perhaps that is where the inspiration came from. They decided to use the carnival-like city of Key West as their model. For a ten-day period in the heart of the summer, Caseville becomes known as Key North and mimics the carefree identity of its namesake.

Caribbean music is everywhere and Jimmy Buffett becomes the national hero. In recent years, the 'Pirates of the Caribbean' movies have served to augment the popularity of the festival. Reggae and steel drum bands are imported and young women roam the streets in grass skirts and coconut shell bikini tops. There is even a parade of tropical fools.

The locals didn't stop there though. In a stroke of marketing genius they targeted one of Jimmie Buffett's most popular songs, "Cheeseburger in Paradise" and named the festival simply "Cheeseburger." The next step was to invite all of the local restaurants and bars to set up cheeseburger stands all over town and compete for the best cheeseburger at Cheeseburger. Now they had very reasonably priced food available everywhere you looked and families could afford to bring all the kids along and feed them for just a few dollars. The crowning gem is the event button that can be purchased at any business in town for just a few bucks and it becomes your admission to your choice of nightly concerts at the band shell in the park plus the daily entertainment throughout the town and on the bathing beach. It's inexpensive but very lively entertainment for the entire family. Due to the affordability and its close proximity to major cities, the Cheeseburger Festival actually grew in popularity as the economy declined. It helped that there were a couple of state parks for camping as well as several county campgrounds and a smattering of privately run trailer parks. It became a high visibility bargain.

Every year it seems that rumors surface that Jimmy Buffett will be making a personal appearance. The fact that Cheeseburger is the largest Parrothead Festival in the country helps to fuel the credibility of the stories. So far he's never showed up but the Chamber of Commerce keeps hoping.

Caseville has a population of fewer than one thousand citizens but estimates of the daily attendance regularly exceeds thirty thousand and well over a hundred thousand visitors are cycled through the city during the ten-day festival. On the day of the parade some estimates exceed fifty thousand tourists. Cheeseburger has become the economy of Caseville.

It was another bright sunny morning and Michael headed out to breakfast and found McCoy waiting for him in the motel dining room, a coffee sitting in front of him and a colorful brochure unfolded on the table in front of him. When Michael sat down across from him, McCoy spun the brochure around and slid it in front of the private detective. McCoy tapped his finger on the brochure. "I don't like the smell of this."

Michael took a few minutes to go over the document, shrugged and said. "Just looks like another summer festival to me. All resort towns have them. Why don't you like it?"

"Okay, I'll spell it out for you. We're investigating a potentially dangerous weirdo who seems to have a shark fetish as well as a facility that's, shall we say 'shark friendly?' His own twin sister, the person who knows him better than anyone is totally convinced that he's just chomping at the bit to raise havoc and start mass murdering his neighbors. And now we find out that we're about to experience a one thousand percent population explosion within the next week or so and it's a giant beach party. And you don't see no calamity hiding in the weeds? Or should I say cattails?"

The waitress arrived with another coffee cup and a pot of steaming Java. She poured a cup and nudged it over in front of Michael. "Same as yesterday?" she asked. Both men nodded and she set her course for the kitchen to order two number-one breakfast specials.

"I'm still not completely sold on the shark theory," mused Michael. "It just seems like such an enormous and complicated project and it would have an extremely high risk of failure. If you want to create total chaos on a large group of people, smart money would be going in another direction like a bomb or poison gas or something that is sure to work. But sharks? Too hit-or-miss for my liking."

McCoy rocked his head from side to side. "Well, you've got a point but, Nah. I think this guy wants something all his own. It's gotta have his signature on it. Something with flair and style. He wants to strike absolute terror into anybody who sticks a toe into any of the Great Lakes whether it's in Caseville or Chicago or Cleveland, Buffalo, Toronto, Ontario, or in Erie, Pennsylvania. He's a fruitcake and those kinds of guys tend to have their own demented form of logic."

Michael smiled. "Oh, I'm not totally discounting your weird theory. As long as his sister keeps paying us I guess we'll keep looking. Which reminds me, I've got to call her today with an update. I suppose we've made a little progress but I expect a lot more tomorrow when we cruise past the place in that sailboat. Deputy Waldecker wants another get together this afternoon to make sure that we've got everything in order for tomorrow."

"How much do you know about sailing?" asked McCoy

"Not much but I don't have to know anything. I'll be down in the cabin taking pictures. How about you? Ever been on a sailboat?"

"Used to race 'em," parried McCoy, "On the Detroit River when I was a kid. One of our neighbors set me up. He was a member at the Detroit Yacht Club and they had a whole class of sailboats just for junior sailors. I was pretty good, too. Won a few trophies. I know it ain't like those big boats but the fundamentals are the same. I'm gonna enjoy myself."

Michael's cell phone rang. "O'Conner Investigations. Oh hello, Miss Prescott." He looked at McCoy who remained silent. Michael filled in Bonnie Prescott on the meetings that they had with the others and briefed her on the results of the fly over and photos. And then he listened for what seemed a long time while Bonnie talked, nodding now and then.

Michael said, "That will be at the Farmer's Bar in Hewellton at six o'clock this afternoon," he rattled off the address, "I'll be sure to keep you informed." When the call finally ended, he closed the phone and put it in his pocket.

"You look upset Mike. What'd she say?"

Michael looked up at McCoy. "She says that she wants to come up here to attend our next strategy meeting. She says that she needs to talk to the sheriff's deputy to make sure that if and when her brother has to be arrested that nobody hurts him."

"You suppose she's having second thoughts?" asked McCoy.

"I don't think so. It sounded more like she felt he was headed for a personal disaster. It's not so strange that she's worried about him, after all they're twins. Got to be rough for her to see what's happening to him. She was kind of crying the whole time."

It was the same group that met at the Farmer's Bar yesterday with the addition of Bonnie Prescott who, after being introduced to everybody just listened for the first part of the meeting.

Dee Phelps was the first to speak. "It's going to be a nice day so I'll be expecting quite a few boats out there. It'll make great cover. It's a popular spot for shallow draft sailboats because there are almost never any powerboats or jet-skis in the area. And Michael, I'd suggest that you wear a dark-colored tee shirt and maybe even a hat. That would make you less conspicuous. I don't think anybody will be able to see you but we might as well be careful."

"Got it," said Michael. "The rest of you guys are all gonna dress like sailors, right?"

"Any idea what you're looking for?" asked Steve, the trucker.

Deputy Waldecker spoke up. "For my part I'd like to find any reason at all to pay an official visit to the property. From what I've seen so far, there's no way I'm going to ever get close without a warrant and I have nothing, no reason at all to convince a judge to sign one except that his sister has a bad feeling about him. As of now there can be no formal police investigation."

"What about that 'Driller' guy and the pickup that was abandoned just outside Brian's driveway?" asked McCoy.

"Turns out that this isn't the first time he's gone missing. I hear that he's having marital problems over his drinking and he pulls these stunts from time to time trying to drive his wife nuts. When we talked to her she didn't want to do a missing person report. She claims he'll likely turn up in about a week, thinks he's with a girlfriend. That would explain the truck being left by the side of the road. In the meantime she'll be keeping an eye on their bank account to see if there's any ATM activity."

"Anybody got anything else?" asked Michael.

After a short silence Bonnie Prescott got to her feet. "I know that I'm the one who started this tempest. You have no idea how much it hurts to have to do what I'm doing. Brian is my brother and the only family that I have. It's true that he has lived a turmoil-filled life but I truly believe that he can't control it. He seems to have an overpowering "me first" attitude but he wasn't brought up that way. There has to be an answer for his behavior but none of us has been able to see it. What he needs more than anything is competent mental health care. I won't pretend to know anything about these strange maladies but I know that assistance is out there. I'm asking you to help me deliver him into caring and capable hands. He wasn't raised to be a monster. He came from the same home that I did so I know that the substance was there. My plea to you is that, when the time comes you'll treat him as a human being and not as some sort of depraved animal. He is the way he is because of some strange disconnect in his mind. And he's my brother. My twin brother."

CHAPTER 28

Maybe it was because of his upbringing but Brian wasn't at all sure how he would feel after being directly responsible for killing two human beings. He had grown up in a loving and considerate household and had been taught moral values by his parents. He thought about the magnitude of what he had done before he went to sleep that night but had been careful to dull his senses with generous amounts of rum before retiring. There was never a doubt that he'd go through with the deed but he was uncertain just how much guilt would clutch him or if he would be buried in remorse. He spent much of the next day replaying the event in his mind and he couldn't get the image out of his head of the two men panicking, their eyes wide with terror as they drew their last breaths on this earth. The more he thought about it, the more it excited him and the less the screaming voices tormented him. He had no trouble sleeping on subsequent nights. No sorrow, no repentance. He liked what he had done.

Brian was at work early this morning. He had moved the barge out of the way and hooked the trawler up to the floating island. He pulled the cattail raft away from the boathouse entrance and anchored it in the channel. Now he moved the barge into position and lifted his newly constructed shark cage off of the grass and slowly lowered it into the water directly in front of the boathouse. He was pleased to see that it lined up nicely with the entry way to the shark pen. This was the riskiest part of the job as far as being discovered went. As long as the portable cage was exposed there was always the chance for another fly over and the whole project would be quite visible from the air. He had to work quickly.

The quarter-inch-thick wetsuit probably wasn't necessary but Brian felt comfortable wearing it even in the tepid waters of the bay. The SCUBA equipment that he used was state of the art and made things a lot easier. He stayed underwater for close to an hour swimming around his shark cage several times as he chained it up to the pen under the boathouse. Transferring the sharks from their pen to the cage was going to be dangerous and tricky but he felt that his plan was sound as long as he paid close attention to every detail. When the time came he'd put some bait near the front of the cage and once the sharks were occupied he'd actuate the quick releases that held the cage to the pen and move the whole apparatus 4 feet forward to give the gate room to swing shut, securing the sharks inside the cage. Once the gate was latched he could disconnect the spring that had pulled it shut and then, when it was time to release the sharks, all he'd have to do would be to pull the rope that held the lock pin in place and the gate would fall open. He would move the fish into the cage at the last minute.

Brian's underwater activities seemed to make the big fish uncomfortable. They kept swimming aggressively in his direction only to have their progress thwarted by the steel bars of the pen. Even though he had infinite faith in the strength of the barrier Brian felt a sense of panic every time one swam in his direction. It was obvious that their homing senses were operating on a high level.

With the cage securely in place Brian repositioned the barge and linked the tow cable to the floating cattail island and slowly dragged it over the top of the cage. Now, with all of the incriminating evidence out of sight, he began to breathe a little easier. He docked the barge and jumped into his little 16 foot runabout so that he could motor out into the bay and have a good look at his handiwork from the open-water side. After several ride-by's, he declared it passable. He knew exactly where all the seams separating the natural vegetation from his artificial implants were and he still had trouble identifying the mooring lines that held them in place. The casual observer would never notice anything unusual.

The next step was to prepare the disguise for the trawler. The old fishing tug was primarily an open boat, its afterdeck resembling a deep cargo well to enable the crew to efficiently deploy and retrieve the hundreds of feet of fishing net. The two big diesels were buried amidships below the deck. The lone piece of superstructure was the pilot house that always reminded Brian of an outhouse.

He had measured it a dozen times but he checked the dimensions again just to be sure. The mounting brackets for the new topside were in place and the anchoring bolts for the wheelhouse were all loosened. It was just a matter of lifting the wheelhouse off of the trawler and replacing it with the superstructure from the old cabin cruiser. The fit wasn't exact but the controls would be in the right place so the boat could be operated normally. It wouldn't pass a dockside inspection but from 50 feet or more away it would look just like one of the thousands of other sport-fishing cabin cruisers on the bay. The disguise would be put in place the night before his plan was to be carried out.

Satisfied that all was ready on the home front, Brian turned his thoughts to the dilemma that Shorty represented. Chances were that Shorty was dead. As a matter of fact, Brian was about ninety percent sure of that. But it was that ten percent of doubt that nagged at the back of his mind. The sharks, in their efficiency, had left precious little evidence of who it actually was that fell prey to them. Logic told him that it had to be Shorty but he would have felt more comfortable if there would have been a wallet or something left floating on the surface of the shark pen. He decided to take one more look inside the crew shack that Shorty had stayed in for a couple of nights.

One of the things that bothered Brian was the absence of any of Shorty's personal belongings in the shack. It's true that Shorty had come here with not much more than the clothes on his back but there should have been at least something. He remembered Shorty having four extra packs of cigarettes that he had picked up in town just the night before he disappeared. He couldn't have smoked them all and it wouldn't make sense to have had them all in his pockets. And then there was the jacket. It had been hanging on the back of the barstool in Miller's Bar when Brian first encountered Shorty and he remembered seeing it draped over the little guy's arm when he climbed into Brian's Durango. It had been around eighty-five degrees on the day when the shark incident occurred. There would have been no reason for Shorty to be wearing the jacket. Something caught Brian's eye. A sliver of white paper was visible between the cushions of the small couch that sat in front of the television. He walked over and tugged on it. It turned out to be the flap of an envelope. It must have been in Shorty's pocket and slipped out when he reached for his lighter or some such thing. He pulled it out examined the contents. It was an overdue notice for a payment to an appliance company. He turned the page over and on the reverse side was the address of Wallace Stueber, more commonly known as 'Shorty.'

Brian checked his watch. He had plenty of time to drive down to Bay City and visit "Heavenly Acres Estates," mobile home development.

CHAPTER 29

Shorty had hoped to be more comfortable sleeping in his own bed but the night had been absolutely miserable. He slept for about an hour and then woke up wide-eyed and shaking. He spent almost two hours peering out between the cracks in the window shades into the dimly lit streets of the mobile home park. A gentle breeze moved the tree branches, heavily laden with summer foliage, from side to side sending frightening shadows skittering back and forth, each one looking like a crouching assassin. He lay down again and tried to sleep but the demons of the past few days kept his eyes wide open. At some point he must have finally dozed off because he jumped up with a start, not sure if he'd heard a noise or whether it was imagined. He repeated his earlier routine going from window to window checking the locks and watching the mercenaries close in. It must have been near six o'clock before fatigue and exhaustion finally took him. Sharon's alarm went off at 7:30. She didn't want to leave him alone but she had four houses to clean in the next couple of days and they desperately needed the money.

Shorty hadn't said a word. He was lying on his side staring at the wall.

"I don't want to leave but I've got to go to work. They're depending on me and we can't afford to have me taking days off. I'll fix you some breakfast before I leave and you can lock things up tight as soon as I'm out the door. I'll knock twice when I get back home so you'll know it's me. I'm sure nobody followed you home. If they did, they would have been here by now. Just the same, I hauled your old baseball bat out of the closet last night and it's leaning up against the wall right next to the door."

Shorty swung his skinny legs over the side of the bed and yawned, "What time you gonna be home?"

"I should be finished by about three and I'll come straight home. You'll be okay. Nobody knows you're here."

"And I'd just as soon keep it that way," said Shorty. "If anyone asks, all you know is that I'm working up north somewhere and can't always get to a phone. You can tell people that you hear from me now and then but don't be specific, tell 'em it's been a few days. And above all don't tell nobody that you seen me. I'm supposed to be dead y'know."

Shorty grabbed his pants off of the chair next to the bed and rummaged through the pockets. He came out with a handful of bills held together with a paperclip as a makeshift money clip. "I think there's over a hundred dollars here. It's the money that Brian paid me. There was more but I spent a bunch on that sleeping bag and other stuff." He handed the money to Sharon.

His wife took the bills from his outstretched hand and put them in her purse without counting them. If it was anywhere near a hundred dollars it would make a big difference in their daily finances. They were used to living on food stamps. She kissed Shorty on the forehead and hustled out to the kitchen to start breakfast. It wasn't much,

Wal-Mart brand toaster waffles and cheap imitation maple syrup but it was the closest thing they'd see to a fancy meal in this house.

Shorty was on his second cup of coffee when Sharon left the house. He bolted the door behind her and made the rounds of the windows once more, rechecking all of the locks and peeking out from behind the shades. The landscape didn't seem as threatening in the daylight. He felt a definite pang of jealousy when he saw three kids riding by on their bicycles laughing and joking. They were so carefree and confident and he was a prisoner in his own home hiding behind locked doors.

Hoping to get at least some sleep he stretched out on the couch and turned on the television. The sound was barely audible so that it couldn't be heard from the outside even if someone pressed their ear up to the door. Shorty had the kind of survival skills that can only be learned on the streets. After all, he had been a bona fide hobo for about five years in his younger days. He rode the rails from coast to coast several times and had lived in hobo encampments in at least seven states. He had been beaten and robbed three times when he was still new at the game but eventually he learned and now he was pretty good at avoiding trouble. Vigilance and awareness were the keys. But this was the first time that he'd ever felt that his very life was in jeopardy. The things that he had seen in Brian's boathouse weren't meant for prying eyes and he knew that just witnessing the carnage was enough to make him a liability. There was no doubt that he represented a threat to Brian as long as he was alive. In spite of the horrible thoughts that swirled in his mind, he eventually dozed off.

A sharp knock on the door jarred Shorty awake. Nobody ever knocked on his door. He was shaking so badly he couldn't even stand. He rolled off of the couch on to the floor on his hands and knees. A second knock came, harder, more persistent. Shorty continued crawling until he could pull himself up to a window that couldn't be seen by anyone standing in front of the door. He was aware of the sound of a car idling just outside the window. As he looked through the small opening at the side of the window shade he could make out the silhouette of a black Dodge Durango. Brian had found him. His heart was pounding. If Brian broke down his door there was no way that he could reach the baseball bat. He needed some sort of weapon and the only thing he could see was an iron sitting in the laundry room. The doorknob rattled and from where he was hiding he could see that someone was trying to open the front door. Sweat was beginning to pour down his face and sting his eyes.

Then he heard voices. He recognized the deep baritone tones of the park manager, a retired Detroit cop who always seemed to know what was going on. "Can I help you?" asked the manager.

Brian answered. "Well, maybe. I'm looking for a guy they call Shorty. He did some work for me and I want to give him his money."

"Shorty's been gone for about a week," said the manager. "I heard that he got a job somewhere up north. Nobody's seen him since he left."

"Ah, that explains why I haven't been able to track him down," said Brian. "Any idea when you expect him back?"

The park manager eyed him suspiciously. There had

been no mention of leaving the money with Shorty's wife. Cops always notice those things and perhaps his old habits were kicking in. "Maybe around the first of the month," he said, "That's when the rent on the lot is due. He always pays me on the first."

Shorty had to smile as he listened to the wily ex-cop. Brian had just basically been told that he shouldn't come back until the first of the month. If he showed up before that, the manager would know for sure that something wasn't right. He relaxed just a little.

The door slammed on the Durango and it pulled away slowing down a few times as it encountered the speed bumps that the trailer park had insisted were needed to slow traffic down. They worked, at least for the Durango.

It was around 3:45 p.m. when Shorty heard the familiar rattle of Sharon's old Ford Ranger as it pulled up in the designated parking spot next to their trailer. There were two soft knocks at the door. In spite of all the recognition Shorty made sure that he could identify his wife before he opened the door.

"So how was your day?" asked a smiling Sharon as she entered the trailer.

"Not so good," replied Shorty, "Brian was here."

"Are you sure? What happened?" Her smile had disappeared.

"It was him all right but Art, the park manager, ran him off. He must have seen Brian come in and followed him here. He handled it great too. Didn't give Brian one piece of useful information."

"But he might come back to talk to me," concern showing in Sharon's eyes.

"That's the thing, Art never mentioned you. Brian still doesn't know that I'm married. He doesn't know about you."

"So what are we going to do?"

"We've got to find another place to live until this thing blows over."

"Well, we can't go to my sister's. She's got young kids and it just wouldn't be right to put them in danger."

Shorty thought for a moment. "What about your brother over in Cass City?"

"You know that I don't get along with him too well. I'm not even sure he'd take us in, even temporarily." Sharon frowned and then said, "Okay, I'll give it a try."

It was dark when they left the trailer park. Shorty hid on the floor of the truck as they slowly made their way out to the main highway. When they were a mile or so down the road he got up in the seat and fastened his seat belt.

"You know something, Sharon?" he said. "You're the best wife a guy could ask for. If we get out of this thing alive I'm going to see a judge and clear up all of those old traffic tickets. Hell, they're mostly defective equipment violations because of all the old junk that I always drove. Anyway I'll pay those old fines and get my license back. Then I'll get a real job and bring home a regular paycheck like a regular husband. I'll start treating you like a real wife and maybe someday we can even take a real vacation."

Sharon didn't say anything. She just looked at Shorty for a long moment and smiled.

When they finally arrived at Sharon's brother's farm near Cass City, they found him in the barn working on a big John Deere combine. He didn't even look in their direction as he said. "You can use the bedroom at the east end of the house. There's no sheets or blankets on the bed. I hope you brought your own. And another thing; there'll be no drinkin' on my property."

Sharon's brother had never married and had devoted his life to sugar beets, soy beans, and field corn. Sharon was quite sure that he had to be a very wealthy man, farming close to thirty-five-hundred acres but he never offered anything for free. Not even to family. Their parents had been poor people, never living above the poverty line. Sharon's sister had married a guy with a regular job as a welder in a small factory and they had settled into a comfortable middle-class life living in a modest-middle class house in a middle-class neighborhood. They had a retirement program, health care insurance, and two-weeks paid vacation. Their kids had ipods and wore Nike's.

Sharon, being the ugly duckling of the family, grew up believing that she would never amount to anything and fulfilled that prophecy by marrying Shorty, a man with similar vision. They lived in a mobile home purchased with the money from an insurance settlement from an incident when Sharon had been walking home from work one night and was hit by a drunk driver breaking her leg and several ribs. The ambulance-chasing lawyer who represented her made enough on the case to buy a hunting cabin on a hundred and twenty acres up north. Sharon's share was enough for a seventeen-year-old house trailer with a non-functioning washer and dryer.

Sharon's brother Bill, on the other hand was a bully who learned to take what he could without regret. There was no doubt that he was a hard worker and as he grew older he was ruthless in his business dealings. Starting out as a hired farm hand, he levered his way into purchasing a small farm and then borrowed agricultural equipment to work the land. After a couple of years he was well-enough-off to lease more acreage and triple the size of his operation. He hired illegals who would work for below minimum wages and he drove them sixteen-hours a day. Bill never went to movies or bars or church. He was obsessed with making money and he was very good at it. In spite of his wealth, he was a totally miserable man. Bill became the poster child for the phrase, *Money can't buy happiness.*

Three siblings, three lifestyles.

Shorty and Sharon settled into the small bedroom. It was even smaller than the bedroom in their house-trailer. There were three other unoccupied bedrooms in the farmhouse and they were all larger and less dreary than the one that Bill had assigned to them. Even Shorty's dull mind recognized the message there.

"We're going to have to figure some way out of this mess," said Shorty. "There's no way I can spend more than a couple of nights in this place. I was more comfortable when I was on the run and sleeping in the weeds with all the mosquitoes."

Sharon wore a defeated expression. She couldn't have known what a cold reception her brother would give them. She decided that they wouldn't even consider using any of the kitchen appliances. It would be fast food brought home in a bag. And watching television was out of the question. It was looking like it would turn out to be a most unpleasant visit.

Chapter 30

McCoy was as good a sailor as he had bragged about being. He knew which sails to deploy, or in sailor's terms, unfurl and which lines went where and what they all controlled. Dee Phelps' eyes said that she was impressed while Deputy Waldecker simply looked amused. Everybody was dressed in nautical-looking gear and it looked quite like a group of pals out for a day of sailing in the light breeze.

As promised, the sky was cloudless and the winds so light that they barely ruffled the sails. But that didn't deter the dozens of diehard sailors who gathered to display their sailing prowess and challenge one another in tests of speed. Most had ventured north from the marinas that dotted the shoreline near the town of Bay Port while a few had sailed southward from Sand Point. Laughing could be heard in the quiet sunshine and soft music floated from the decks of a few boats. It was a party atmosphere on Wildfowl Bay.

Michael O'Conner was ready, batteries fully charged in both of his cameras and fresh memory cards installed. At the moment he sat with the others in the afterdeck as the sailboat known as *The River Dancer* moved into position.

"I know this part of the bay pretty well," commented Dee, "I sail here often. I'm pretty sure I know the place you're talking about. There are only a couple of occupied homes in the area and only one looks well cared for."

"If you're one of the regulars around here, that's a good thing," commented Michael. "If he's seen the boat around in the past, it won't set off any alarms if you happen to run a little close to his property."

Dee turned to Michael. "We do it all the time to catch the offshore breezes. I recognize every boat that's out here. I'm sure Brian does too and he's used to seeing all of them." She changed the subject. "We're almost there. You might want to get down below and get everything ready. I'll have McCoy or our truck-driving buddy relay our position to you as we approach."

Steve Kraus spoke up. "I'll do it. I need some kind of job around here I love playing this spy stuff."

Michael made his way down the short three-step ladder and retrieved his camera from the forward bunk. He removed the lens cap and positioned himself in front of the open sliding window. He waited. "Two hundred yards," came the call. "One fifty. One hundred. Fifty." Michael turned on the power and gazed at the viewfinder. The sailboat slowed as it moved past the entrance to the first channel. Michael snapped about twenty pictures as they drifted by. For a moment the cattails obscured the view but then he had a clear view of the house and all of the outbuildings. Everything looked peaceful on shore. He could see a black SUV parked next to the house. The trawler was tied to the dock and the barge was about 50 feet away at the other end of the pier. The two boats had reversed positions since the fly over if he was remembering correctly. The old cabin cruiser rested in its cradle but now the ladder had been moved to the stern. Everything about the stately old homestead had an innocent flavor to it. The place just didn't have the threatening look of an evil empire. As they glided past the second channel at the north end, Michael shot another twenty or so quick photos before they reached the state-regulated wildlife sanctuary that surrounded the old Prescott mansion.

The sailboat cruised the area for another two hours approaching Brian's hideaway from a dozen different directions offering a variety of camera angles. When they finally set course for home, Michael emerged from the below deck cabin drenched in sweat and smiling. "We got some great stuff here. I don't know if anything is going to help but every inch of that place has been recorded."

Steve spoke up. "When I visited this place a month or two back, we were going to check out the diesel engines on that barge. Mr. Prescott had called the mechanic and asked him to come out. He met us up at the house and wouldn't let us anywhere near the dock. Said he didn't need a mechanic anymore because he had sold the barge 'as is' for salvage. We asked if we could just have a look at it but he hustled our asses out of there. He looked pretty nervous. As I think back on it now, my being there was a surprise to him and that might be what bothered him. I introduced myself and I'm pretty well known around here. If he's heard about me and knows who I am, that might be reason enough for him to not let me get any closer."

"What do you mean?" asked Dee.

"Well, if he's hiding something, he sure doesn't want any high-profile citizens discovering it. Here's what I'm talking about. If some anonymous diesel mechanic uncovers some dark secret, getting rid of him might not be a problem. But if a guy like me who owns a thriving local business, has relatives on just about every block, and sits on the board of the county business development association turns up missing, people are going to notice and ask questions. The best solution is to avoid allowing me any access to anything. That way I can't be a threat." Steve uncapped a root beer.

The sleek sailing vessel moved effortlessly and silently into the slip and was secured to the pilings in all four corners thanks to the sailing expertise of McCoy and Dee Phelps.

Deputy Waldecker said, "Dee and Steve and I are headed over to the drive-in for a burger. Anyone want to come along? We can compare notes." Everyone agreed.

As they sat at the outdoor picnic table devouring hamburgers and thick chocolate malts, Steve offered, "Well, the first thing I noticed is that the crane barge that was supposedly sold for salvage is still there and he's been using it."

"How do you know that?" asked Michael.

"The last time I saw it there was a drag link, a dredging tool attached to the end of the cable on the crane and now there's a hook on it. He's been lifting something heavy and the barge has moved. It's at the other end of the dock." "Yeah, I noticed that the barge had been moved too," said Michael, "Just since our fly over the other day."

"We've still got the same problem though," said Waldecker, "There's nothing even remotely suspicious or illegal about any of this. If we ever plan on landing a warrant, we're going to need a whole lot more than we've got. The best chance that we have for anything is if Driller's wife would agree to file a missing person's report and even then it'd be pretty iffy that a judge would sign a warrant based on the fact that the subject's car was found in close proximity to Brian's property."

"I thought it was actually on his property," said McCoy.

"Michigan Department of Transportation claims a right of way to 30 feet from the center of the road on State highways," said Waldecker, "That pickup was technically still on the road."

"So that puts us back to square one," added McCoy

"Well, I've still got these pictures to go through," said Michael, "and if I see anything with any meat on it, maybe I can find a way inside without going through the legal system. Maybe I can find a way to get myself invited in somehow."

"Good luck with that," said Steve, "Well, I gotta hit the road. I've got a business to run." He climbed into his Chevy pickup truck and cranked the engine over.

"You'd never know that man was rich, would you?" said Dee as the three-year-old pickup pulled out of the parking lot. "He's as regular a guy as anybody else around here. I went to high school with him. He hangs out and parties with the locals. Never forgot his roots. Not many like that."

"Self made man?" asked Michael.

"Absolutely," answered Waldecker.

Back at the motel, Michael downloaded the day's pictures, filing them in categories along with the photos taken from the airplane. His pictures confirmed that someone had indeed changed the tool that hung from the crane boom on the barge. At least they had a time window for that activity.

He compared the pictures and was sure that he could see a slight discrepancy in the landscape. The area that he concentrated on was the suspected *floating island* that he had identified in the first series of pictures. When he began to lay out and examine today's shots from the many different angles of approach it soon became clear that some of the cattails were about two inches taller than the others and that they were all condensed in one area, the same area that he had been looking at as being artificial. They fit that piece of the grid perfectly. Now he had proof. Well, sort of. But what good was it?

Brian sat in his living room trying to make sense of the things he'd seen out on the bay today. There were a lot of sailboats out there today and he was pretty sure that they were just the regulars. He had been watching through the powerful spotting binoculars that had been designed for spying on rocky mountain goats at distances exceeding two miles. He could clearly make out the features of every person on every boat. One of them, the girl whom he'd seen many times in the past and she had a couple of new faces aboard and they were all looking in his direction every time the boat was in sight. He was sure that there was another person on the boat as well, someone who was purposely staying below decks and out of sight. He could see movement in the cabin and at one point it looked like a single lens looking back at him, possibly a telescope or powerful camera lens. It was probably nothing but paranoia, but it was different and it worried him. The name on the boat was The River Dancer. He made a mental note to find that sailboat and check it out. He noted that it departed in a southerly direction, most likely to a marina in the Bay Port area. It should be easy to find.

As he drove through Caseville that morning he noted that all of the banners touting the summer Cheeseburger Festival were in place and their exotic messages in vivid colors were screaming at every vehicle that passed through town. The beer tents were going up and the cheeseburger grills were being unloaded all over town. Only a few days left and there wouldn't be a motel vacancy within sixty miles. The festival was scheduled to start this weekend.

Brian hadn't really given much thought to his future after his assault on Caseville but he had taken the precaution of moving large chunks of his fortune to untouchable offshore banks and had paid big money for a phony identity that was sophisticated enough to include a passport. He was sure that his name would eventually be connected with what was about to take place but had figured he would be well out of sight before that happened. Now he was beginning to wonder. The boats in the bay had been somewhat unnerving. Out of all the sailboats playing their usual games out there, only one seemed to be paying special attention to him and that boat had strangers on board. And maybe at least one of them had a special interest in him. What if someone knew what he was up to? But how could they know? The only answer that popped into Brian's mind was Shorty. If that little guy was somehow still alive, he'd be the only one with eyewitness evidence. But was he still alive? Brian had no proof that he was. That nosy mobile home park manager down there where Shorty lived had made it sound like nobody had seen Shorty, but he'd become a formidable barrier. Brian would have to find another way to determine for once and for all whether

Shorty was dead or alive. The unknowns were beginning to drive him crazy and the voices that screamed in his head were gaining volume. He had no plan.

CHAPTER 31

The gentle knock on Michael's door startled him. He approached the door cautiously and peeked out through the blinds. A young lady stood in front of his motel room door.

"Hello," said Michael, "What can I do for you?"

"Hi there, I'm the assistant manager here and I have to inform you that this motel is booked up solid during the Cheeseburger Festival so the rooms that you and your partner are in won't be available after tonight. There is one option though. One of our beach cottages has just had a last minute cancellation but if you want that unit, you'd need to rent it for the full ten days and it's rather expensive. It does have two bedrooms and a kitchen though, so you could split it with your partner."

"How expensive?"

"It's $250 a day, $2500 for the full festival." The young assistant manager looked like she was expecting a physical assault because she stepped backwards as she quoted the price.

"I don't suppose there are any other local vacancies," said Michael.

"Nothing this side of Bay City."

"I'll give you a tentative okay on the cottage then but I can't confirm it until I talk to my client. I can give you an answer as soon as I hear. How long can you hold it?"

The young lady consulted the notebook in her hand. "I can give you until eight o'clock tomorrow morning. Is that okay?"

"No problem." The manager smiled and hurried back in the direction of the motel office.

Michael left the door partially open and went back to his computer where he was studying his pictures and added a note to call Bonnie to the growing task list on his small desk. He had barely sat down when another knock drummed on his door. This one was accompanied by the robust voice of McCoy. "Yo, Mike."

"Come on in. I want you to look at something." Michael turned his laptop so that McCoy could examine the screen.

"Okay," said McCoy, "I see a close up of the house. Good-looking place, three stories and lots of gingerbread, probably worth a few hundred grand. So?"

"Take a good look at the corner window on the second floor," said Michael.

"Oh yeah. I see. There's someone up there and they're checking us out with a pair of binoculars. Standing back away from the window so that we can't see him. That telephoto on your camera is really something. Think he's made us as detectives or is he just being curious?"

Michael shrugged. "Could even be a voyeur. I would imagine that all kinds of things go on out in those sailboats. No way of telling for sure. But to be on the safe side, I'd suggest that we assume that he knows somebody is interested."

"Not to change the subject but I assume you know that we're being kicked out," said McCoy.

"Oh right. I've got to call Bonnie about that. If she

wants to keep us in town it looks like it's gonna be another five hundred bucks. Geeze, I hate to throw more expenses at her. She's been so understanding up to this point."

Michael dialed Bonnie's number. They spoke for just a few moments and Michael told her about the festival and the housing challenges that it presented. He ended the conversation with a "I can't thank you enough, goodbye."

McCoy had a big grin on his face. "So she said go for it, eh? We're gonna be roomies for a week or so. It should remind you of your old college dorm days. I just hope you don't snore."

"You've got a private room, just shut the door."

Michael's phone rang. "Oh hi, Dee. Wow, I didn't even notice. Probably because I had that big lens on there. Okay, I'll swing by and pick it up.

"What was that all about?" asked McCoy.

"Seems like I left my camera case on Dee's sailboat. She said that she left it on the afterdeck on the helmsman's seat. Wanna go for a ride with me while I pick it up?"

"Sure thing, Landlubber. I'll show you where the helmsman's seat is."

Brian was in his third marina this afternoon and he had finally spotted the River Dancer. There was nobody aboard but he decided to sit at a safe distance in his vehicle and keep an eye on it for a while. He had been watching from a spot three docks away for a little over a half hour when a Chevy Trailblazer wheeled in the driveway. It headed straight for the first dock and came to rest directly in front of the slip that embraced the River Dancer. The man who jumped out of the driver's side was an unfamiliar face to Brian but the guy who climbed out of the passenger door was the man that Brian had seen this morning on the sailboat that kept cruising by his front door. Perhaps the other man had been the one who stayed out of sight below decks the whole time.

As Brian watched, only one of them went aboard the sailboat and it looked like he was only there to retrieve some forgotten article because he didn't stay for more than a couple of minutes. Neither man looked in his direction as they got back into the Trailblazer and headed for the exit. Brian dropped the Durango into gear and followed them out staying a safe distance behind. Within a few miles Brian had managed to let another vehicle slip in between them. It didn't surprise him when the Trailblazer led him all the way to Caseville and pulled up in front of a beachfront motel. He had been far enough back that by the time he drew even with them they were entering the second room from the corner of the building on the first level. Again, neither even glanced his way.

Now he knew where they were staying but it didn't do much to relieve his anxiety because he still had no idea who they were and why they would be interested in him. His thoughts went back to Shorty. If that guy was still alive and had spilled his guts to the authorities there would have been a SWAT team beating down his door and not some civilian-looking sailboat hanging around the bay. None of it made any sense. If there was something that was making the local Sheriff's Department nervous why hadn't they at least contacted him? And then he remembered the pickup truck that had been in the ditch just a few feet from his driveway. Maybe that was it. Maybe they were all looking for the driver of that truck. He hadn't seen anything on the local news or in the papers about anybody missing. Perhaps the family was keeping the cops out of it. But still, that truck showing up just after the sharks had attacked and gorged themselves on some unfortunate human being was enough to make him nervous.

The closer he got to putting his plan into motion, the more paranoid Brian became and the more he was visited by the screaming voices. First it was that diesel mechanic that dragged his boss along and then there was the whole Shorty fiasco, and Brian had no idea where that stood. And that airplane that flew close to his place still bothered him. Next it was the abandoned pickup truck and this morning there were people spying from a sailboat. If it had been only one or two things he might have been able to pass them off as coincidences but this was just too many. There had to be something more to it. But why was everybody keeping their distance? He had no idea who these people in the sailboat were or what they wanted but their interest in his place was more than casual. Brian had to concentrate to calm himself down. He was beginning to unravel. The puzzle was just too much for him. He was terrified of being caught. Killing two men didn't bother his conscience, it actually stimulated him. But if he was arrested and thrown in jail before he could execute his plan, according to his logic his life would be wasted. He couldn't bear the thought of rotting away in a prison full of common criminals. It was maddening. Brian began having trouble sleeping again. He spent most of the night in a cold sweat, dozing for a few minutes at a time.

The sunrise didn't bring him any relief. There were still no answers. He decided that his best course of action would be to just keep tabs on those two guys that drove that Trailblazer. They were the only tangible thing he had. If he could figure out who they were, things might become clearer.

CHAPTER 32

Ever since they got home from the marina Michael had been trying to reach Sharon Stueber to see if she had heard any more from Shorty.

"You really think he's in any way tied to this thing?" asked McCoy.

"I honestly haven't a clue but I know that I'd feel better if I knew he was safe at home. It's just that his wife—and she's a pitiful and defeated person—well she doesn't seem to know where to turn and Shorty is her entire world. She doesn't want to go to the police because Shorty doesn't trust cops, so where can she go? I feel really sorry for her. And now it's like she's dropped out of sight too." Michael tried the number again.

McCoy sat on the edge of the bed. "I'll get the guys back at the office to run a check on this Shorty guy. You say his real name is Wallace? We'll see if he's got a sheet and go from there. And tomorrow is moving day but I've got nothing else on my calendar so we can run down and knock on his door if you like."

"Yeah, it would give us something to do tomorrow," said Michael, "I'd feel guilty taking Bonnie's money if we just sat on the beach all day. I'll run Sharon's number through the reverse directory and see if I can come up with an address."

"And I'll see if we can move into our new digs tonight so that we can get an early start in the morning."

The motel manager gave McCoy and Michael permission to move into the new cottage suite that evening provided that they pay the extra day's rent. It took less than forty-five minutes to clear everything out of both rooms and move it all into the new suite. McCoy pointed out the fact that both bedrooms had generous waterfront views so they wouldn't have to arm wrestle over who got the best room. Michael was pleased to see that there was both a desk and a table so that the two of them could use their laptops at the same time. "I guess the extra money that Bonnie has to shell out for this room isn't such a waste after all."

McCoy piped up. "By the way, the guys weren't able to get much on Shorty. All he's got is a handful of traffic tickets and the only one that weighed anything was an impaired driving citation that never went to court. The judge decided that there was something wrong with the ticket and he threw it out. Shorty doesn't have a driver's license because he owes about a hundred seventy-five in fines. Other than that, he's clean."

Michael joined in. "I've got an address, too. It's a trailer park just inside the eastern city limits of Bay City. Already got it in the GPS. It says that it's less than fifty miles from here. I figure that we can leave here around 6:30 in the morning, stop somewhere for breakfast and be there before Sharon leaves for work. She still hasn't answered the phone but if she's got caller ID, she'll know it's me calling because I've called her before. She might just not want to talk to me."

"Who could blame her?" grinned McCoy.

It was almost 6:45 a.m. by the time they got on the road so they decided to grab a quick breakfast at a drive-thru. They pulled in next to the trailer at slightly before eight o'clock. Michael frowned at the absence of Sharon's Ford Ranger in the trailer's designated parking place. He decided to knock on the door anyway. He was standing on the small porch when a man pulled up in a retired Chevrolet police cruiser. There were still faint outlines where the Sheriff's Department vinyl stickers had been removed. The man even looked like a cop when he stepped out of the car and moved in the direction of Michael.

McCoy, still sitting in the passenger seat of Michael's Trailblazer noticed something familiar about the man. He opened the door and stepped out. The man stopped in his tracks and studied McCoy for a long minute. Finally he said. "Your name McCoy?"

"Yep. Where do I know you from?"

The man smiled. "Detroit P.D. Third Precinct. Retired. Got a nasty divorce after I left the force so these days I'm working here as the manager. I'm almost back on my feet now so hopefully soon I'll be moving on to those golf courses and sandy beaches with Tiki bars that I dreamed about when I got my thirty years in."

"I think I remember you now. Your name is Blake. Sergeant if I recall."

"That's me. What can I do for you guys?"

Michael had come down from the porch. "We're trying to find the guy who lives in this trailer. Can you help us?"

"Shorty sure has become a popular guy these last few days. Can't rightly say where he is though and I have no idea when he might be coming back. Haven't seen him in at least five or six days. And now his wife has disappeared too. She was here yesterday because I saw her come home from work. But then she drove out a little later and hasn't come back. As far as I could see she was alone in the truck but I suppose somebody could've been hunkered down in the passenger's seat. They've lived here for quite a while. They were here when I got this job. I'll say that Shorty goes away for up to a week at a time every so often but I've never seen her go away for even a single night. They're actually pretty good tenants, one of a very few couples that always get their rent in on time and never cause any problems. Keep their place up. Stay to themselves a lot."

"What did you mean about getting popular?" asked Michael.

"There was a guy here yesterday saying that Shorty had done some work for him and he wanted to pay him. I thought that was kind of strange because I pegged Shorty for a guy who worked for cash only and under the table. Those kind of arrangements are always pay as you go. The guy was acting a little spooky too. I sort of gently ran him off without telling him anything."

Michael excused himself and ran back to his vehicle where he retrieved a photo from his briefcase. "Could this be the man?" He extended the picture to the park manager who studied it for a minute. "Yes sir, that's the guy. This picture looks to be maybe eight – ten years old but it's the same guy."

Michael and McCoy looked at each other. "You got a key to this trailer?" asked McCoy.

"Pretty sure I do," answered the manager, "Most of the residents leave one with me in case of emergencies. I seem to remember Mrs. Wallace giving me one and asking me not to mention it to Shorty." He shook his head and smiled. "Is this an official investigation? You have a warrant?"

Michael dug out one of his business cards. "No, I'm a private investigator looking into the activities of the man whose picture I just showed you. His sister hired me. We think that Shorty may have done some work for this guy and may have accidentally seen something that he wasn't supposed to see and now the guy in the picture is after him. We think he's on the run."

"What would you expect to find inside the trailer? I could get in trouble letting you in there."

McCoy spoke up. "We'll back you up a hundred percent. We're checking on the welfare of the people who live here. And we won't disturb anything while we're inside. They'll never know we were here."

The manager stood with his hands on his hips staring at the ground. "Well, okay. I'll be back with the key in a minute." He jumped into his car and made a U-turn.

When they got inside the trailer Michael was surprised to see how neat and clean the old place was. Then he remembered that Sharon made her living as a cleaning woman. Something looked out of place in the living room. There was a cheap camouflage print backpack draped over the back of the one of the two couches in the room and its contents strewn over the seat cushions. "Looks like he's been on a camp out," said Michael pointing to the tent and camp stove.

"Maybe that's how he stayed out of sight between Wildfowl Bay and here," said McCoy. "Hiding somewhere away from the roads during the day and traveling at night."

"I'd look at it as evidence that he's been here," observed Michael, "How else would you explain this stuff?"

A short tour of the rest of the trailer told them nothing new. They thanked the trailer park manager for his help and headed back north.

"Looks like Brian Prescott is definitely tied in with Shorty," said Michael as they drove back toward Caseville. "His wife was in a near panic when I first talked to her and then she settled down after Shorty called home. Then it was panic again and now a vanishing act."

"They're running and hiding," commented McCoy.

"And scared," added Michael, "Did you see that baseball bat next to the front door?"

CHAPTER 33

Brian didn't really like guns, they left way too much evidence whenever they were used. But he had a 9mm Glock in his glove compartment in case things got really out of hand. The black Dodge Durango was parked in the middle of a long row of cars near the back of the motel parking lot. Brian had been sitting there since about ten o'clock this morning waiting for the Trailblazer to show up, and after a mostly sleepless night he was now having trouble keeping his eyes open. He didn't like this spy stuff at all but it seemed to him that he had little choice. He absolutely had to find out what these two guys were up to. He still held a tiny bit of hope that it was all his imagination but there seemed to be too many coincidences for it to be anything other than enemy action.

If he could hold these guys at bay for just another week, his mission would be accomplished and he would simply disappear. He envisioned the scene where he would get his boat as close as he dared to the designated swimming area of the county park and then open the big gate on the back end of the cage. As soon as the sharks were in the open water he'd activate the spring-loaded pullers that would jerk the bungs out of the buoyancy barrels allowing them to fill with water. At the same time he would release the tow hitch. The shark cage would then slowly sink to the bottom and the trawler, then free of the extra drag, would be able to maneuver at a respectable pace. He knew that he wouldn't have too much time to actually enjoy the turmoil and confusion once he released the sharks and they had identified their targets but he figured that he'd be able to hang around for fifteen minutes or so and watch the action through his binoculars. He hoped that he'd be close enough to hear the screaming. Then he'd have to hightail it for home and jettison the cabin cruiser disguise and reinstall the old pilot house on the trawler making it look like a commercial fishing boat again. He rehearsed the scenario over and over in his mind as he sat waiting for those two mysterious operatives to return to their rooms. They were already gone when he got here this morning and at first he wondered if they had gone to breakfast but if that were the case they should have been back by this time. Now he began to wonder if they weren't back aboard that sailboat giving his house and property another maybe even closer look.

There was a different vehicle parked in front of the room that he'd seen them enter yesterday afternoon but that didn't necessarily mean anything. It was well past lunchtime and he was just about ready to give up his surveillance when he saw them come rolling into the parking lot. The Trailblazer seemed to slow a little as it passed the corner room but then it made a left-hand turn and disappeared around the end of the building. Following them at this point was out of the question. Brian would be much too visible. He'd have to wait and see if they had just parked in back and would walk to their room. But he waited almost another half hour and they didn't reappear. By now

Brian was wondering if they had made him and were playing mind games with him. It was maddening. He never dreamed that his plans could be discovered and of course there was no firm evidence that anybody had figured out what he was up to. He guessed that nobody knew exactly what he had in mind but somebody was pretty sure that he was up to no good. That's what puzzled him. Why would anybody suspect him of anything? It was as if someone had inside information or someone knew him well enough to be concerned.

And then a thought came to him. His sister. He felt that Bonnie had always looked down on him, regarded him as dirty and evil. It seemed like she traveled through life doing virtuous things like helping the less fortunate while he was the consummate playground bully. She had always come across as saintly while he was considered the sadistic one. If there was anybody in the world who would suspect him of wanting to do great harm to anyone it would be Bonnie. She never trusted him. The more he thought about it, the more sense it made. She almost went crazy when she discovered that he had put that gate up across his driveway. She was particularly upset that it couldn't be seen from out on the highway. She accused him of hiding it so that he wouldn't look like he was covering something up. It was probably that gate that tipped her over the edge. He knew that she feared he would do something terrible someday and maybe now she was sending the bloodhounds to see what was transpiring in his corner of the world. It was like an epiphany. That had to be it. It must be Bonnie. He needed to find out for sure if it was she who sent up the alert flares and hired somebody to breathe down his neck. Maybe he could charm the information out of her and change her mind. That was a tactic that had always worked when they were kids.

Brian didn't bother packing a bag, he wasn't planning to stay overnight. He'd never been to Bonnie's new home on the other side of the thumb near a place called Lexington, a little ways north of Port Huron. All he knew was that her house was basically on the same state highway as his, the difference being that she lived on the shore of Lake Huron while his frontage was technically on Saginaw Bay. It was about a two and a half hour drive according to the information on Brian's GPS.

It was just about dinner time when Brian pulled into his sister's driveway. He was pleased to see her Corvette sitting in front of the garage. He had decided to make it as friendly a visit as he could. After all, he needed information not tears.

He pushed the button for the doorbell and could hear the chimes ringing inside. It only took a few seconds for Bonnie to pull open the door. The look of horror on her face told Brian just about everything he wanted to know. "Hi Bonnie," he smiled.

"Oh hi. I didn't expect you, I mean it's been months since we've even talked. Why don't you come in and you can fill me in on what's been going on with you." Bonnie stepped back and held the door wide open for her brother to come in. He followed her through the house and she opened a sliding glass door that led to a large limestone deck overlooking a mirror-smooth Lake Huron. A few hundred feet offshore the 858 foot ore carrier, the *Roger Blough* plied its way northward, its bow wake creating the only ripples in the water They would find their way to shore in about twenty minutes and bubble up on the beach, then the water would be dead calm again. She offered him one of the upholstered patio chairs and gestured toward the very tropical looking Tiki bar off to one side. "Can I get you anything to drink? Cocktail? Beer? Soft drink?"

"No thanks. I'm fine," answered Brian, "I was just in the neighborhood looking at a boat I'm thinking about buying and thought I'd stop by for a look at your new house. It's quite a palace, by the way. How big is it?"

Bonnie seemed to have regained her composure. "It's about 3500 square feet. Three bedrooms, a study, five and a half baths, dining room, that kind of thing. I wasn't really looking for a place this sprawling but when the realtor showed it to me I immediately fell in love with it. And the beach is fabulous. I can show you around if you like."

"Maybe later," said Brian, "Seems like a huge house. Why so big? You planning on getting married or something?"

"No. Not even a boyfriend in the picture. But you should talk, the house you're living in is a lot bigger."

Brian smiled a relaxed smile. "But it was Grandma and Grandpa's place, I didn't pick it out. You've got a lot prettier view here."

Bonnie looked a little more serious. "Are you planning to keep the place? It's so... isolated. It's got to be lonely out there.

Brian shifted in his chair. "Sometimes I think about selling it but if I did, the government would buy it and turn it into a breeding ground for ducks. I don't think that's what Grandpa had in mind. I've got kind of a sentimental attachment to it. If I decide not to live there full-time I'll probably still hang onto it as a place to get away. You know kind of a refuge. The isolation can be nice sometimes but I worry about security too. I mean what if somebody decided to break in while I was away? They could clean the place out and there would be nobody to stop them."

"But you've got that big gate across the driveway," protested Bonnie.

"Well, it looks good but it won't stop anybody who's determined to get in. It's mainly there to keep teenage vandals out. I only installed it because I found some graffiti spray-painted on the boathouse when I first took the place over and I figured that the gate would put an end to that sort of thing but now I'm not so sure."

"Did somebody get past it?" asked Bonnie

Brian scratched his head. "I'm not convinced that the driveway is the problem. Lately I've seen people in boats checking the place out from the water side. As a matter of fact, I kinda get the feeling that I'm personally being watched, too."

"Really? That's got to be creepy," Bonnie raised her eyebrows in a surprised look.

"That's what I thought too. Do you have any idea who might want to follow me around?"

Bonnie stiffened. "How would I know anything about that? Why would you even ask me that question?"

Brian shrugged. "When I was younger I used to do a lot of stupid things that seemed to worry you as well as mom and dad. But that was a long time ago and those days are far behind me. I've grown up since then. Looking back, I can completely understand why you guys were so concerned. I just thought that you might still possibly look at me in that light."

Bonnie seemed to be studying the big lake freighter as it quietly knifed through the deep blue water. "At one time I was very concerned about you. For a while you seemed to be on a path to self-destruction. Right up until you left for college, but that was a long time ago. I haven't thought about it at all lately. But I'm glad to hear you say that you've changed direction."

"No question," replied Brian, "Now I'll take that tour of your new house."

The trip home gave Brian time to reflect on the visit to his sister's home. She had answered the door with terror in her eyes. There had to be a reason for that and he knew her well enough to believe that a feeling of guilt had a hand in driving her fear. In spite of her denial Brian was reasonably sure that she was behind the sudden interest that strangers were taking in his activities. He hoped that he had sounded convincing enough when he told her that he had turned his life around. It seemed as if she believed him or at the very least that she doubted herself. She was acting much more at ease by the time he gave her a hug and left. Feeling that he had some answers allowed him to relax a little. Of course, there was still the dilemma of Shorty but Brian knew that he'd have to handle his challenges one at a time. For now, he tried to put it out of his mind. He needed rest. Perhaps the watchdogs would be called off. Maybe he could even sleep tonight. If the voices would only stop screaming.

CHAPTER 34

Shorty offered to help his brother-in-law around the farm in exchange for the use of the cramped little room that he shared with his wife. He was busy cleaning up a large shed that was used for storing agricultural equipment. It was pretty obvious that his benefactor didn't have the same flair for neatness that Sharon had. The place looked as if it had never been cleaned. He figured the job would take several days. He had found a large folding table leaning up against the back wall and the first thing he did was clean a spot for the table and then set it up. From that point forward any tool, any piece of pipe, any nail, any lock washer that he encountered while cleaning would be placed on that table so that he couldn't be accused of throwing away some valuable object. There were hooks on one wall that had obviously been designed for hand tool storage but they were all empty and the tools that were supposed to be kept there were scattered throughout the building. Shorty was doing a thorough job that included clearing all of the cobwebs from the light fixtures and washing the windows. He was making a sparkling trail through the building. The weather was hanging around in the upper-eighties and Shorty was drenched in sweat but he didn't mind. Anything was better than sitting in that dreary room all day.

From time to time Sharon's brother would pop his head in the door and look around. The first time he peeked in Shorty yelled a greeting to him but he didn't bother to respond. Nothing in his demeanor indicated whether or not he was pleased with what he was seeing. He just looked around and then withdrew.

Shorty worked straight through the day. Not even taking a lunch break. He had his water bottle in his back pocket and there was a spigot over in the barn so that he could refill it once or twice a day. He didn't quit until he heard Sharon's old truck roll into the driveway. She got out of the truck with a McDonald's bag in one hand and a couple of milkshakes in the other. They wandered over to the old apple orchard on the other side of the house and sat in the tall grass, shaded by the trees. The light breeze still carried the sultry humidity of the day but it still felt somewhat refreshing. This was the most pleasant part of the day and the only time that Shorty could truly unwind. They had their burgers and fries in silence and then treated themselves to nice rich milkshakes that cooled them in the heat of the day. They packed all of the wrappers and empty cups back in the bag and Sharon would dispose of them in the trash cans at work tomorrow. They didn't want to be accused of adding to Sharon's brother's garbage.

When they were finished Shorty laid down on his back with his hands folded behind his head. "Y'know I wouldn't mind living in a place like this if things were different. Maybe if it was like our land and we were making a living here. I've worked on a lot of farms in my life and I know how to do just about everything. Yeah, it'd be all right."

"I know," said Sharon. "But we've got to face what we're struggling with. We can't stay here and we can't keep running. Sooner or later you're going to have to deal with what you saw in that boathouse. The longer you put it off, the worse things are going to be."

Shorty rolled onto his side and propped himself up on his elbow. "I've thought about that a lot. I can't get it out of my mind. I can still hear that guy screaming. Even though there was no possible way I could have helped him, it still seems as if it was somehow my fault. But you're right. I've got to do something about it. It's just that I'm scared."

They sat in the orchard until the sun went down and then walked back to the house. Shorty took a quick shower and changed into clean clothes. When he wandered downstairs to the living room he found Sharon in quiet conversation with her brother. They stopped talking when Shorty walked in the room. "Am I interrupting something?" he asked.

"No, no," answered Sharon, "We were just talking about how the farm is doing. It's time for bed anyway. Tomorrow's Saturday and I've got two churches to get cleaned up for Sunday services. Gotta start extra early tomorrow so I'd better get some sleep."

When they got up to their room, Sharon began crying. "Sometimes he's such a jerk," she sobbed, "He wanted to know what kind of trouble you were in and why we couldn't go home."

Shorty paled. "So what did you tell him?"

"I told him that it had nothing to do with the police. That you hadn't broken any laws or anything. I told him that there was this man who was just very mad at you and we didn't know why. You never done nothing to him. The guy is just crazy or something. I couldn't think of nothing else to say to him."

"And what did he have to say about that?" Shorty sat on the bed.

"He said he didn't want no lunatics chasing you around his house. He gave us three days and then, we've got to be out of here. But if anybody shows up here looking for you before that, we're gone immediately."

Shorty put his hand on Sharon's shoulder. "We'll think of something. I'll go tell the cops what I saw if I have to and take my chances. You just get a good night's sleep and clean those churches in the morning. Maybe Sunday we can take a ride somewhere, go on a picnic or something. We can probably do some planning if we just get away to some place that we feel comfortable. We'll figure it out. I promise."

CHAPTER 35

McCoy was sitting in a plastic chair on the small deck of the cabin that he shared with Michael. The bay was calm and teeming with kids, mostly teenagers swimming, playing catch with nerf footballs and floating around on assorted brightly colored inflatable plastic toys. Six girls in bikinis were playing volleyball on the beach while a dozen or so drooling high school boys sat watching. There had to be close to a hundred kids on the beach and nearly that many more in the warm water of the buoy-marked swimming area. A few boats and jet skis roamed the waters farther offshore.

Michael walked out the door and plopped down in the chair next to McCoy.

"Just got a call from Bonnie Prescott. She wants another meeting tomorrow night but she doesn't want it to be here in town. I suggested that Farmer's Bar out in the middle of nowhere. She said that would be okay but she wants us to bring as many of our allies as we can muster."

"That may not be easy," answered McCoy, "The big Festival starts the day after tomorrow and most cops of any flavor may not able to get away. You better call 'em and find out."

Michael made his calls to Dee Phelps, Deputy Waldecker, and to Steve Kraus, the trucking company owner. To his surprise they all agreed to be there tomorrow at six o'clock in the evening.

McCoy nodded. "Did you tell Miss Prescott about the Shorty connection with her brother that we discovered today?"

"Nope. Didn't have a chance, it was a pretty brief conversation. She said that there might be some changes and she'd fill us in when she gets here."

"Hmm," said McCoy. "Think she's getting cold feet? Changing her mind about finding out what the hell he's doing?"

"Honestly, it almost sounded that way," said Michael, "I got the impression that she'd talked to him recently. But she told me once that he can be a very manipulative guy. I wonder just how susceptible she is to his persuasion. I guess we'll find out tomorrow night."

"Look at the bright side," said McCoy. "The rent is paid on this absolutely premium cabin for the next ten days. If the job gets cancelled, we've still got a gorgeous vacation in front of us."

"You've got a good point about us still being on the clock. That means that our checkbook is still open so I think I'll reserve an airplane for an early-morning fly over tomorrow. We don't have to do any low altitude stuff so he won't get spooked. My camera lens can still bring in a decent close up at 1000 feet in the air. I just want to see if anything has changed since the last time we looked." Michael began dialing the phone.

The earliest that Michael was able to book a charter flight was eleven o'clock. He wasn't happy about the late start but decided to go along with it anyway. Besides, the pilot was a buddy of Deputy Waldecker's and Michael didn't have to explain much. They'd only be airborne for a couple of hours and that would still give them plenty of time to get to the meeting with Bonnie. He should even have a chance to go over some of his new photos.

The sunrise the next morning promised another beautifully clear day with the weatherman predicting no end in sight to the ideal summer weather. The farmers might have preferred a little rain at this time of year but the next weather system capable of producing even a light shower was still west of the Rockies. That suited the festival promoters just fine. The small plane cleared the end of the runway at eleven o'clock sharp and banked westward toward Saginaw Bay.

Michael sat in the co-pilot's seat with his camera in his lap as he chatted with the pilot. "Do you know the area pretty well?" asked Michael.

"Sure do. I even know the property that we're going to have a look at. Me and a couple of my buddies used to do lawn chores for old man Prescott when we were kids. Great guy, always paid us well and his wife was ready with a big dish of ice cream as soon as we finished the job."

"Did you ever get to know his grandchildren?"

The pilot scratched his chin. "They were a lot younger than me, I can't recall ever seeing them but Mrs. Prescott talked about them all the time. I hear that the place belongs to the grandson now."

McCoy spoke up from the rear seat, "How much did Deputy Waldecker tell you about our mission?"

"I pretty much know what it's all about. I used to be Waldecker's boss over at the Sheriff's office. I called him last night after I talked to you and had him fill me in. I just retired last summer so I sometimes feel like I'm still on the job."

"Then you know what we want," said Michael, "We don't want to arouse any suspicion so we'd like to be high enough when we pass over his place. We don't want it to look like we're checking the place out."

"Well then how about if I approach the place from the land side a little bit to the south of his place and then kinda bank to the right and follow the shoreline north. That way we'll be tilted at a good angle for your camera as we fly by in front of the property. I'd suggest that we only make one pass to minimize the chance of making him nervous. I'll keep the speed down and you should be able to shoot lots of pictures."

"Sounds okay to me," said Michael, "We're a little pressed for time anyway, besides I've already photographed the entire layout. These pictures will just be for comparison."

The view was breathtaking as they approached the bay. The sun was only slightly behind them and it reflected off the light ripples in the water illuminating them like so many diamonds skipping over the quiet bay. From their altitude it was easy to identify the underwater rock shelves that dropped off to deep water, changing the color from blue to black. Michael could see the house and all of the outbuildings now and was busy clicking away with his camera, swinging the unwieldy lens back and forth in the cramped cockpit. He didn't say a word but continued to take pictures throughout the entire maneuver until he was twisted around as far as his lap belt allowed, trying for just one more shot. "Headed home now?" asked Michael.

The pilot just nodded.

They got back to the motel at just about two in the afternoon and McCoy ran into town to pick up a pizza for lunch while Michael loaded the memory card from his camera into his laptop. By the time McCoy returned all of the photos had been downloaded and categorized, ready for comparison to the earlier shots.

"Have a look at this," said Michael as he turned the screen toward McCoy. "Don't put your greasy fingers on the screen though." Michael was watching the olive oil from the pizza running down McCoy's fingers as he stuffed his mouth with the pepperoni-covered pizza.

"What am I looking for?" asked McCoy.

"See that old cabin cruiser sitting in the cradle in the first set of pictures? Now check out the way it looked this morning."

McCoy leaned in closer. "I'd say that he's taking it apart."

"That's how it appears but he's sure going about it in a strange way. He has removed the entire deck in one piece including the cabin roof and fly bridge. It's sitting there on the ground next to the boat. It doesn't make any sense to do it that way. Smaller parts would be much easier to handle. He must have used the crane on his barge to lift it off"

"Maybe he wanted it in one piece," pondered McCoy, "That's about the only thing that would make sense."

"But why?" asked Michael.

"I guess that's for us to figure out." McCoy reached for another slice of pizza.

Michael moved on to a different file folder. "I found something else, too. See this thing that I told you that I thought was a floating island? When you compare the first photo from the other day to the picture I took this morning, you can see that it's moved probably a foot or more. In the first picture the edge of it is lined up precisely with the wall of the boathouse but in today's shot it extends beyond that wall."

"Hmmm, curiouser and curiouser," said McCoy.

"And one other thing, although I don't know if it means anything." Michael opened another folder. "See this truck here? In the first picture it's hard to tell just what kind of truck it is. At first I thought it might be a dump truck. The pictures that I took from the sailboat didn't really shed any more light on it. But this morning we came in from a different angle with the airplane and I got a pretty decent shot of the whole thing. It looks like a tanker truck with a recirculating filter system. The kind that they use for hauling live fish. Except that the tank on this one is built different. It hasn't got the big valve on the back for emptying it. Looks more like an oversized hatch. Same arrangement on top. Weird."

"Like maybe it's made for sharks?" asked McCoy

Michael gave him an annoyed look.

"Can you zoom in on that picture taken from the rear of the truck" asked McCoy.

Michael did his best but the photo became quite grainy the more he enlarged it.

McCoy sighed, "Well I can't exactly make it out but I can tell you pretty much for sure that it's not a Michigan license plate on that truck. From the colors I'd say Pennsylvania."

Chapter 36

Dee Phelps and Deputy Waldecker were waiting when Michael and McCoy arrived at the Farmer's Bar. Steve Kraus, was right behind them and Bonnie arrived within the next fifteen minutes. The usually quiet bar was bristling with people this afternoon. The bartender explained that it was the Friday fish fry that brought all of the customers to this little four-corner town. Next week would be even crazier because it would be in the middle of the Cheeseburger Festival that would be taking place a scant seven miles away in the waterfront community of Caseville. The staff was hustling to get the remodeling finished on the dining annex so that they could handle the anticipated crowds. In the interest of privacy, the bartender offered Bonnie and her group the use of that room provided they didn't mind the odor of fresh paint and tile adhesive. Bonnie accepted without hesitation.

As soon as the door was closed and she was reasonably sure that they were out of earshot of the crowd, Bonnie began, "I suppose you're all wondering what's on my mind this afternoon. Well, I'm not exactly shutting down the operation but I'm asking you to evaluate everything you've seen and uncovered so far and advise me. I'm interested in your thoughts and opinions too."

Michael was the first to speak. "Has something changed

that has caused you to doubt your original concerns? Do you want us to back off?"

"Backing off might be just a little stronger than I want. Let's just say I'm concerned with how close you are right now."

McCoy chimed in, "What does that mean? How do you know how close we are? I mean we don't even know how close we are."

Bonnie took a deep breath. "Brian stopped by to visit me and we talked. He seems convinced that someone has been watching him but he doesn't know who or why. Right now he's not even positive that it isn't his imagination. But he feels the heat. The fact that he actually came to my house tells me that it's really bothering him. I suppose that the feeling of being watched would make anybody uncomfortable whether they have anything to hide or not."

"Did he say what it was that made him think he's being watched?" asked Michael.

Bonnie looked at the ceiling for a moment. "Well, he said that there were signs everywhere. He mentioned something about boats out in front of his place. I'm guessing that he's referring to that sailboat that you guys talked about at your last meeting.

McCoy spoke again. "To be honest, Miss Prescott we've been finding things that point to the possibility that your brother could be involved in some troubling activities. We haven't had the opportunity to bring them all to your attention but we were hoping to be able to do that tonight."

"Very well," replied Bonnie, "Lay it on me."

Michael cleared his throat. "I suppose I should begin with the surveillance photos that I've taken from both the air and from the water over a period of about four or five days. It looks as if your brother has been constructing some camouflage landscape features such as a floating island made of cattails and swamp grasses. And then he's been doing some strange alterations to an old cabin cruiser that is sitting on his property."

Bonnie's eyebrows went up. "Cabin cruiser? Are you sure it isn't the fishing trawler that you're looking at? I don't think he has a cabin cruiser, at least I don't ever recall seeing one."

"Oh, it's a cabin cruiser all right," answered Michael. "A very old one. Looks like it's all wooden construction. He seems to have lifted the whole top part of the boat off and it's resting on the grass near the dock. He's gone through a lot of bother to keep that upper portion intact."

"Well, it's all interesting," responded Bonnie. "But there doesn't seem to be anything criminal about it. I must admit though that the idea of a floating island might be a bit disturbing."

"There's more," said Michael, "And the rest is particularly bothersome. There's this guy from Bay City who seems to be more of a barfly than anything else. Anyway it looks like he may have hooked up with your brother as a day laborer working on one of his boats. According to the guy's wife, her husband took the job on the spur of the moment and headed straight to Brian's place up there on the bay. The lady said that she heard from him a couple days later and that he claimed he was happy with the job and was hoping to make some big money. She didn't get any details though. A day or so after that the husband calls back in a panic and all out of breath. Says something about running for his life and then the line goes dead. We were able to track down his address but when we got there we found that both the husband and wife are missing and that Brian had been to their place looking for them."

"Can you be sure of any of this?" asked Bonnie.

"We're still trying to check things out. That's why you haven't heard about this development sooner. The manager of the mobile home park where this couple lives is the one that identified Brian, but that's all we have right now. Anyway he's helping us out and says he'll keep us informed if anybody shows up.

"When Brian visited me he made it sound as if he was just hanging around our grandparents' old house doing little fix up jobs and deciding whether or not he wanted to live there permanently. He didn't mention fixing up any old boats although he did say that he was out my way looking for a boat to buy. But maybe that was just an excuse for him to be in my neighborhood. I'd like to be kept in the loop on this itinerant worker that was supposed to be doing things for Brian. I actually came here prepared to lower the intensity of this probe that we're doing but now I'm not too sure what I should do."

McCoy joined in. "Miss Prescott, there may be absolutely no connection here but your brother's college roommate told us that he had an abnormal fascination with sharks. Have you ever seen that side of him?"

Bonnie shuddered and after an uncomfortably long pause she said, "In a way, I think I may have. When he was in high school he used to keep a lot of creepy pets. I can remember that he would go out in the springtime and catch garter snakes. He kept them in a big aquarium. Then he would go frog hunting and he'd bring the frogs home and throw them in with the snakes. Then he'd put a cover over the top of the aquarium so that the frogs couldn't jump out and he'd sit there watching for hours and giggling whenever a snake caught one of the frogs and swallowed it alive. He always bugged my parents to buy him some piranhas from the local exotic pet store. I know that the only reason he wanted those fish was so that he could throw live mice and other little animals into the piranha's fish bowl and watch them attack. Sharks would only be a grown-up version of that same fantasy and I'd hate to think what he'd want to feed them. I'm just glad that they're salt-water fish."

McCoy was writing notes. "But do you think your brother would actually pursue anything that crazy if he had the means?"

"When he stopped by my house we talked a little about his strange behavior back when he was young. He didn't try to deny any of it and he told me that he had definitely moved past that phase of his life. He certainly sounded sincere. I'd like to believe him."

"When I first took this case I think I said that I hoped to find nothing," said Michael, "And so far there has been nothing concrete but we've been uncovering so many unusual things that it makes me want to keep going. I have lots of unanswered questions here."

"But are they simply curious questions or do you really suspect that Brian is planning some diabolical scheme?" asked Bonnie.

Deputy Waldecker stood up. "May I add my concern?"

"Go ahead," said Bonnie.

"Thank you. A few days ago, actually it was the day of

our last meeting, I was called to sign off on an abandoned vehicle so that it could be towed from a location less than a hundred yards from your brother's driveway. The owner of that pickup truck still hasn't surfaced. We don't have an official investigation going on because his wife won't file a missing person report. But the guy has definitely dropped out of sight. I've talked to a few of his friends and nobody has seen him. That worries me."

Bonnie sank into a chair. "I need a few moments to think." After a brief silence she asked, "I'm convinced that it could it have been you people who made Brian nervous by spying on him from that sailboat. Am I right?"

"I'm sure it was us," said Michael, "I actually have a picture of him checking us out with a pair of binoculars from inside his house. So yeah, it was probably us."

Bonnie sighed. "Well then let me ask you to do this. I agree that there are many good reasons to keep watching him. After all I'm the one who started all of this and I know what it's like to worry about what he might do. But we've alarmed him now so it won't be as easy to keep tabs on his comings and goings. Can you give him more space? So far he doesn't seem to be aware that there are actual law enforcement people involved, even if you are doing it on your own time. I view that as a plus and I don't mean for you to let up, just don't crowd him so much. Would it compromise your exercise?"

McCoy answered, "Not at all. Your request is completely reasonable. There are lots of things that we can do from a distance. Besides, our local peace officers are going to be awfully busy with the Cheeseburger crowd. But on the other hand, I don't want to let go of this one. If your brother is suffering from some sort of mental illness or behavioral disconnect, he needs intervention. I still think it's wise to keep him under some sort of surveillance."

Dee Phelps spoke up. "Miss Prescott, I don't want to unduly alarm you but Mr. McCoy's comment about the sharks was quite legitimate. What many people don't know is that there is one particular species of very dangerous shark that does quite well in fresh water such as we have right here in this bay. The alarm went off for us when it was discovered that it was that same breed of shark that your brother studied with great scrutiny in college. I am a shark expert and my only reason for being involved in this case is that there is a possibility, albeit remote, that your brother is raising and harboring sharks at his residence. I'm not trying to alarm you as this thought is based solely on circumstantial evidence. I must admit that it's one hundred percent speculation at this point. And I need to add that the behavior patterns of this particular species of shark are highly unpredictable, making for an uncertain result of any conceived plan. I'm sure that your brother knows this as well. But it needs to be investigated as long as there is even a remote chance."

"Of course, public safety will always be my primary concern," said Bonnie. "And I'm not canceling anything. I'm just asking if there's a way to do this thing without him feeling threatened."

"We'd like that too," said McCoy. "Just how threatened does he feel? Is he pretty positive he's being watched or is he just worried that he might be under surveillance?"

"I got the feeling that he's not entirely sure what's happening," answered Bonnie. "He wasn't specific about anything but he mentioned that he was more concerned about his security on the bay side rather than any threat from land."

"How about from the sky?" asked Michael. "Did he say anything about aerial fly overs?"

Bonnie thought for a second. "No, he never mentioned anything like that."

"How long have we got before you pull the plug?" asked Michael.

"I'm not putting any time limits on it," answered Bonnie. "If my brother is up to something malicious, I couldn't live with myself if I didn't do everything in my power to stop him. But I simply don't know. His past behavior says he's quite capable but maybe I'm just over reacting to that menacing gate that he's put across his driveway. He gave me a plausible explanation but, coming from him, I have trouble believing it. I'd just like an answer one way or another. I'd like to thank all of you for your sincere efforts and I intend to pay all of you. Mr. O'Conner and Mr. McCoy are full-time investigators and the rest of you will be compensated for whatever hours you put in."

Steve Kraus stood up. "Miss Prescott, there's no need to pay me anything. Your detectives didn't hire me, it was actually a bartender who suggested that I might have something to offer. I'm as worried about the welfare of the community as you are and I'd just as soon contribute whatever I can as a concerned private citizen. I'm not a professional, I'm just along for the ride. Besides, I kinda like hanging out with Dee here." He had a big smile on his face.

CHAPTER 37

McCoy wandered into their small living room after his morning shower and found Michael hunched over his laptop banging away at the keyboard. "What's got you so lathered up this beautiful morning? It's not even eight o'clock. Playing a video game or something?"

"I'm just trying to comply with my client's wishes," shot back Michael.

"Such as?"

"Well, I'm investigating from a respectful distance. Instead of hounding Brian, I'm looking for possible incriminating connections," said Michael.

"Would you mind explaining that?"

"I decided to humor you and follow up on your totally ridiculous and far-fetched shark theory. I'm checking out and cataloging all of the shark dealers that I can find."

McCoy laughed. "Seriously? Shark dealers? You mean there is such a thing?"

"Sure is," said Michael. "Dozens of them. Most of 'em sell the little aquarium type but there are a few here that specialize in the full-size ocean-going models. Even bull sharks."

"Now you've got my attention," said McCoy, "Need any help?"

"Probably can use some assistance interviewing these

guys once I've got them all organized. Looks like most of them run pretty tight businesses with lots of restrictions and requirements for buyers."

"I can understand that," said McCoy, "Who'd want a bunch of sharks turned loose in your local swimming pool?"

"Actually, it's the other way around," said Michael, "They appear to be more concerned about the welfare of the sharks. They want to make sure that the buyer can provide a certain-size aquarium with properly monitored environmental conditions, adequate nourishment, et cetera, et cetera. Evidently they don't want their sharks abused."

"Heaven forbid," added McCoy, "I wonder how complete their sales records are. Wouldn't it be nice if we could trace a mess of sharks to this guy?"

"I guess it would answer a bunch of questions and it would certainly make our job easier. It might even be enough to get us a warrant. But I've got to believe that Brian would be more careful than that. If he has evil intent he won't want to be discovered. He'd be operating under an alias for sure. I'd say that what we'd better be looking for is a sizable sale of mature bull sharks to a single party. I'd be willing to bet there won't be a whole lot of transactions like that."

"You're probably right," said McCoy. "I'm hoping that it pans out. I'm absolutely convinced that it's going to be a shark caper. You get your list together and I'll help with the leg work."

Within an hour Michael was able to compile a list of over a dozen businesses whose exotic aquarium dwellers included large sharks. He made an index that included addresses as well as phone numbers. He printed it out and then offered to buy breakfast in the motel restaurant.

"Generous offer," said McCoy, "Considering that Bonnie is picking up the tab anyway."

The two men strolled through the motel parking lot heading for the restaurant. Today was the first day of the Cheeseburger Festival and things were getting busy already. The lot was filling up with cars even though check-in time was still four hours away. Neither Michael nor McCoy noticed the black Durango sitting in a corner out near the road. The man behind the wheel was paying careful attention to them though. He was still sitting there when they emerged from the restaurant forty-five minutes later. Both were dressed in tropical-looking bathing trunks, colorful shirts and deck shoes. They looked very much like any of the tens of thousands of tourists who would be descending on this normally peaceful little town over the next ten days. Brian Prescott took the small digital camera out of his shirt pocket and snapped more than a dozen photos before they rounded the corner of the building and disappeared.

It was going to be another hot one and the weather forecasters claimed that there was little relief in sight. The next chance of precipitation wasn't even on the radar yet. Michael cranked up the air conditioner a few notches as they walked in the door.

Wiping the sweat off of his forehead McCoy said, "You know with this slowdown in our investigation, we might even get a chance to spend some time on the beach, As a matter of fact, I'd say that we'd better check out the big bathing beach at the county park. We haven't even seen it yet and if this guy is planning an amphibious attack, that's the most likely target."

Michael looked at him and smiled. "I suppose you're right."

By around eleven o'clock in the morning they had spoken with all of the aquarium suppliers on their list. The detectives had been asking for information on sales within the last twelve months. Some of the dealers were very helpful, providing the facts while they were on the phone and a few said they'd have to check their records and get back later. One outfit said they didn't share any information without a warrant. McCoy put an asterisk next to their name and made a note to call the Detroit P.D. to see if some of his buddies back at the home office could run a screen on the place.

From what they'd been able to gather, bull sharks were in moderate demand for many municipal aquariums. And there were a surprising number of private aquatic museums buying them as well. Well over a thousand bull sharks had made their way into a free-lunch welfare existence in the last year. Animal activists would view them as captives but the sharks probably didn't mind it a bit when their meals were delivered on a regular basis. It looked like it was going to be a much bigger job than Michael had imagined when he first thought of the idea.

Making sense of the sales figures was going to require a system that could find a unique connection leading to a single buyer. The problem was that Brian was plenty smart enough to use multiple identities. The financial data might provide that link but those records were protected by confidentiality laws. Michael would have to find another common denominator. He picked up his cell phone and dialed Dee Phelps number.

"Officer Phelps, Michigan Department of Natural Resources. How may I help you?"

"Hi Dee, this is Michael O'Conner. I have a question for you."

"Go ahead."

"It's about bull sharks. Would they be okay in fairly cold water? Say like the temperature of the bay in like April?"

"Well, they've been found pretty far north in the summer, around this latitude a lot but I'd say that they wouldn't do well in this area much earlier than mid-April and even that might be pushing it. It's different every year depending on the severity of the winter. The ice would have to be off the bay and they'd need at least a couple of weeks for the sun to bring the water temperatures up."

"Hmmm. Okay, thanks. That's a big help.

"No problem," answered Dee and she hung up.

"Okay, McCoy, we're going to focus our inquiry on sales going back four months from right now. Our shark specialist says that it'd be risky throwing them in water that's too cold. At least that should narrow it down."

McCoy nodded and kept working on his grid.

As the day wore on, it became obvious that narrowing the window didn't help much. It seemed as if most transfers of live sharks took place during the summer months. They're shipped in tanker trucks that are unheated and so water temperature becomes a consideration during transport. They needed to find another similarity.

He decided to cull out all of the aquariums that were

owned by municipalities. For the time being he continued to include all of the theme parks. It wasn't a whole lot better. The numbers were still overwhelming.

In frustration, Michael went back to the photo galleries that he had compiled from all of their spying trips. Going through all of the folders he settled on the pictures of the truck that he had seen from the air. It was definitely a tanker truck and it looked like it had been custom-built. The cargo tank was like nothing Michael could ever recall seeing. The difference was in the size of the hatches. Almost the entire rear end of this tank was covered by what looked like a Navy submarine hatch about 5 feet in diameter, plenty big enough for a full-grown shark to swim through. As much as Michael doubted McCoy's shark theory, he kept coming up with more and more evidence to support it.

It was almost six o'clock in the evening when Michael realized that the dealers would have charged a fee for delivery. And if Brian was the actual customer he probably would have wanted to avoid the intrusion of a delivery driver on his property. If he was buying sharks, he would have almost certainly insisted that he pick them up himself. That's what the tanker truck would be all about.

The information that the dealers had sent to Michael didn't contain any financial information so he couldn't tell which sales included delivery. He dug out his list of dealer contacts and began dialing phone numbers.

After another frustrating half hour he turned to McCoy and said, "All I got was recordings at every one of those places and it seems like they all operate the same; five days at regular business hours, half a day on Saturdays, closed Sundays. And today is Saturday so it looks like this phase of the operation is on pause for a day or so."

"So it looks like we've got a well-earned day off coming tomorrow," said McCoy. Unless you want to use the time reconnoitering the city bathing beach."

Michael grinned broadly. "Have you got bikinis on your mind or something?"

CHAPTER 38

"I can't find a damned thing," shrieked the man in the denim shirt, "I shouldda knowed better than to let that little bastard loose in here. He's got everything screwed up. Nothing is where it belongs. He was just supposed to sweep the floor, dammit."

He looked at the back wall. All of the rakes, shovels, pitchforks, and hoes were hanging from clips arranged by type of utensil and length. The big sledge hammers and axes sat in a line neatly underneath them. Along the side wall was a long folding table stacked with paint cans, small hand tools, spare agricultural machine parts, and oil cans, all neatly organized. Items that were too large or heavy to sit on top of the table were lined up according to size on the floor beneath it. Two pallets in the corner contained bags of cement and fertilizer. The floor was immaculate and the interior of the building was very bright, brighter than he could ever remember because all of the burned-out light bulbs had been replaced and the dust washed off of all the others.

Sharon's brother was stomping around, working himself into a frenzy trying to find a good reason to evict his ne'er-do-well sister and that worthless husband of hers. Worn out from all of his antics, he finally ended his rant and stood in the middle of the building breathing heavily with his hands on his hips. He did a three hundred and sixty 360 degree rotation as he stood there and had to admit, if only to himself, that the building hadn't looked that good even when it was new. Shorty had done a much better job of cleaning the place up than even the builders had when they finished the original construction. There was no cement dust on the floor and no small sawdust piles in the corners. He stepped out the door of his tool shed and walked across the barnyard. He started all three tractors one at a time and parked them in a neat row up against the outside wall of the old weathered barn. The cleanliness bug might be contagious, he thought. As he looked up at the bare grey wooden planks of the century-old building, he briefly considered how nice the place would look if the barn had a new red paint job. Shorty could probably take care of a project like that in a couple of weeks and he'd probably do a better job than the professional painters. Then he shook his head and said out loud, "No way. They gotta be out of here in a couple of days. They ain't nothing but trouble and I got all the problems I need."

Walking toward his house he noticed that Sharon's old truck was parked respectfully out of the way on the gravel apron of the driveway. He could see Sharon and Shorty sitting among the apple trees in the orchard 100 feet or so beyond the house near the wheat field. It looked like they were quietly chatting, Shorty sitting on the ground with his arms wrapped around one knee rocking gently back and forth. For a moment he thought about going over there and giving them some grief so that they'd feel even less welcome than they already did but then he weighed the effort that Shorty must have expended cleaning the tool shed and decided to cut them some slack. He turned and went into the house.

"Have you been thinking about what we're going to do?" asked Sharon, "We can't stay here much longer."

Shorty sighed. "I've got to do the right thing. I'm going to have to go to the police. I can't think of anything else to do. Your brother gave us what, two more days? I'll do the best I can. I'll keep hammering my brain for answers but right now I can't think of another way to go. I'm still not sleeping at night and every time I hear a car coming down the road, I hide until I can see what kind it is and who's in it. I can't live this way. It just ain't right."

"There might be another way," said Sharon, "That young private detective who talked to me sounded like he knew a lot about how the cops worked. And he was investigating a guy who really sounds like he might be the same guy who is after you. If we could get someone like him on our side it might just help a whole lot."

Shorty stopped rocking. "How much did he tell you about the guy he was checking up on?"

"Well," Sharon said, "He was some guy who lived in a really secluded place on Wildfowl Bay and he had a couple of old boats. At least one of them was a commercial fishing boat. I think he said that the other was some sort of work boat. Anyway the guy he was talking about sounded like he might be real creepy. He said that he might be doing some things that were, you know, outside the law."

"Boy, that sure could be Brian," commented Shorty, "Sounds just like him and it sounds just like his place. Did he say what kind of illegal things he thought that this guy was into?"

"I don't think that he could give me any details. You know how all of those privacy things are these days. But if it sounds like the same person who's after you, I'd say it's certainly worth a shot."

"Hell yes," replied Shorty, "This puts a whole new spin on things. If I had known all this a couple of days ago, things might have been different." He stopped and reflected for a minute. "But probably not. I never really stopped shaking until we got here, wouldn't have listened to you. I couldn't have thought straight if I tried. But now I think I'm on the right track. Tomorrow is Sunday and we've got to be out of here before Wednesday so I've still got a couple of days to figure out if it's really the right way to go. I sure hope it is. It would be a huge load off of my mind and I could get my life back. It would be just like starting all over from the beginning and this time I'll do it right. I'll treat you like the princess that you are."

Sharon with the flat hair, 30 pounds overweight, and flour-sack housedress smiled.

CHAPTER 39

McCoy was working his way through the open face ribeye sandwich. He stopped to take a sip of his milkshake. "Who wouldda ever thought you could get this good of a meal at a little restaurant that sits right on the beach?" He gazed out at the expansive bathing beach that was rapidly filling with sun worshippers and families with seemingly dozens of kids following each couple. There were beach balls and umbrellas everywhere and the air was filled with happy sounds. The swimming area was crowded with plastic float toys and an occasional genuine automobile inner tube, an item that might soon be on the endangered species list.

"I had no idea this place would be anywhere near this big," said Michael. "As a matter of fact, it's a whole lot bigger than the bathing beach at Belle Isle in Detroit. There's room for thousands of people here."

"And there will be," The voice came from the waitress who had served them their sandwiches, "The crowds just get bigger as the week goes on. And if the weather holds like they expect it to, we're gonna set records this year. We do over sixty-five percent of our annual business in this ten-day period so it means a lot to us."

McCoy shook his head and turned to Michael. "Since we've got all day, you want to check out the whole waterfront? The stuff like fishing piers and marinas?"

"Sure. Why not?"

As they pulled into the public boat launch they noticed a particularly imposing rig backing its trailer into the water. It was a four-wheel drive one-ton Dodge pickup truck with monstrous tires. It had a very businesslike brush guard mounted over the winch on the front bumper and on the door in bold letters it said "State of Michigan." Underneath were the words "Department of Natural Resources." A familiar figure hopped out of the door wearing a very official-looking uniform including the nine-pound leather harness that carried the Glock, the Mace, and the handcuffs. Dee Phelps, in spite of her diminutive frame, formed an imposing figure in that getup. She recognized the two private detectives instantly and waved, brandishing her best smile.

"Need some help with that?" yelled McCoy.

"Nah, I do this alone all the time. These outfits are built for solo launching."

McCoy and Michael just watched as she easily slid the 20 foot pursuit boat with its huge outboard motor into the launch slip. She threw a line over the piling and jumped back in the truck depositing it in the parking area. When she returned to the waterfront she said, "Hop aboard. We're not leaving the harbor. I've just got to get this thing moored in case we need it this week." The two men jumped in the boat and rode the short distance to the dock marked: Private. Authorized Personnel Only. There was one other boat tied up there and it was marked Huron County Sheriff Search and Rescue.

After securing the boat McCoy remarked, "That

certainly makes me feel a little better. It's good to know that we've got some means of protecting the bathing beach."

"The Caseville Police Department keeps a boat here as well. Right now it's over by the park patrolling the bathing beach, keeping the jet-skis out of the swimming area. And then there's Steve too," said Dee, "You know, the guy who owns the trucking company. He's right over there on Sand Point just a few minutes away."

"Yeah, but he's not a cop," said McCoy.

Dee hopped up on the dock. "True, but if we need to control sharks swimming in these waters, he's the guy I want. He was a three-time intercollegiate rifle champion and a finalist for the Palma trophy for rifle shooting. It doesn't get any better than that. If we have to take out a target from the deck of a rolling vessel, he's the guy I'd want with his eye to the peep sight."

"He's quite an impressive guy," said McCoy, "Along with his other accomplishments I'd say he's done a bit of sailing in his day. He seemed to know his way around that sailboat of yours pretty well."

"He should," laughed Dee, "He's sailed it a lot. It used to be his. I bought that boat from him a couple of years ago and I'll be paying him for a couple of more years before I can really call it mine."

"Have you got a minute or two to answer a couple of shark questions?" asked Michael.

"I suppose but I can't hang around too long," answered Dee.

"I'm just curious about their habits and tendencies. I still can't take this shark theory too seriously but I know next to nothing about sharks," said Michael.

"To begin with, they'd have to be bull sharks in order to survive in these waters. Bull sharks are usually solitary hunters but have been known to work in pairs. They like to eat every day but can go for short stretches, maybe two or three days without food and then they'll begin going after one another. Their diets include just about anything they can swallow including other sharks."

"You mean they don't swim in schools?" asked McCoy.

"Not generally, they're usually solitary hunters but it happens sometimes. There's nothing in their nature that actually prevents it."

"How much damage would, say a half dozen bull sharks be able to do if they were turned loose over there at the bathing beach?" asked McCoy.

Dee looked at the ground and shook her head. "It's hard to say. Each one would seek its own target so I'd say that the impact could be significant. As many people thrashing around in the water as there are today, the sharks could easily become confused and strike out in all different directions. With conditions as they are right at the moment and if they were sufficiently hungry, you could easily have twenty or more attacks to deal with and I'm sure at least some of them would be fatal. That's why, as remote as the chances are that anything like this could happen, I can't just brush it off. I mean, look, after Katrina, Lake Pontchatrain down in Louisiana had a serious situation with bull sharks that were swept in by the hurricane. It caught those people by surprise and I don't need any of those kinds of surprises. I don't really expect anything but I've got to keep my eyes open."

CHAPTER 40

The sun was scorching hot on Brian's back as he labored over the bolts that secured the tiny pilot house to the deck of the trawler. Back at his own dock now, he had begun his day early, running the trawler over to the gas dock in a marina twenty miles south of his home. With the diesel tanks topped off, he now had a considerable range available to him but he had only a short trip planned. He was still on schedule but just barely. It seemed like everything was taking longer than it should. It was Sunday already and the big Cheeseburger Festival was in full swing. There were only seven days left and, according to the weather reports, Wednesday, parade day, was suppose to be blistering, in the upper 90s possibly even reaching a hundred degrees. Wednesday was his target day. The traffic passing his driveway on its way to Caseville had increased more than tenfold. It didn't even let up at night. The flavor of urgency fueled Brian's appetite. He needed to pace himself or he knew that he'd begin making time-consuming mistakes. The pressure was mounting. And the screaming voices were louder than ever. He imagined his blood pressure soaring as he worked. He wiggled the crowbar one more time. There, it was finally loose. The old pilot house had been coated with plenty of bedding compound to prevent water from leaking inside back when it had been installed many years ago. The result was almost the same as if the deck and the wheelhouse had been carved from one solid block of wood. But now it was free and he could hook up the slings and lift it off with the crane. Soon the old trawler would be taking on the appearance of an even older cabin cruiser. A poor man's yacht.

With the pilot house now sitting on dry land, Brian turned his attention to mounting the upper portion of the old cruiser on the deck of the trawler. He had measured everything over and over and was sure that it would sit right in place but he couldn't be comfortable until he actually saw it. His hard work was rewarded with an easy fit of the cruiser's superstructure over the helm of the commercial fishing boat. It was simply resting in place right now; nothing was bolted down yet but he wanted a good look at it so he shut down the crane and walked back up toward the house so he could see what it looked like from a distance. A broad smile broke out across his face as soon as he turned in the direction of the dock. "Perfect," he said.

Brian spent the rest of the afternoon fastening down the phony top section of the boat and then mounting four downriggers and six fishing rod holders on the transom. The finishing touches would be the tall, whip radio antennas that completed the charter sport-fishing boat image. When the work was complete, Brian entered the control station and found that he could stand at the pedestal that held all of the engine and steering controls and look out the cabin windows with a clear view in all directions. This was going to work just fine. Actually it was better than expected.

It had felt good to be able to work outside without the

feeling that he was constantly being watched. There had been the usual compliment of sailboats on the bay today but the River Dancer was not among them and none of them had taken on a threatening posture. Just the normal kids showing off their seamanship skills. The lack of the surveillance threat pretty much convinced him that it was indeed his sister who had put the spies on him. He'd think of some way to deal with her later.

Some of Brian's earliest memories were of his mother carrying Bonnie and making him walk as they browsed the aisles in the department stores. He thought about the look in his sister's eyes as she gazed down from her lofty perch, admiring all of the shiny trinkets that were on shelves that were too high for him to see over. She was allowed to take it all in while he had no idea what she was even looking at. It seemed unfair then and it still seemed unfair now. Bonnie always got special treatment while he felt as if he was always just pushed aside. Bonnie never appeared to notice. She just took things for granted as if she was entitled, never even thinking about Brian's feelings. As a child he was too introverted and self-conscious to ever complain. He simply kept quiet and let it fester, his irritation manifested in disdain for his sister. By the time they were old enough to start school, a small degree of hatred was beginning to creep into Brian's character. And by the sixth grade it was full blown. But still, Brian's personality was such that he didn't outwardly express his rage. Things only got worse as they got older and Bonnie blossomed into a very pretty and popular young lady while Brian, in spite of his athletic build and natural agility, became branded as a hopeless nerd who barely, if ever, spoke and never seemed to smile. His demeanor had a repulsive effect on his peers and he had no success at all developing friendships. As far as he was concerned, a lot of it was his sister's fault but she was simply a part of a bigger problem. The main culprit was the community and the culture that it embraced. It was all so false and so repressive.

Making waves was not a trait of the Prescott family and so Brian had suffered in silence. It was only after going away to college that he felt as if he'd slipped the restrictions and bonds of his ancestors. Being emancipated from family traditions provided him with a freedom that he'd never felt before. Now he could express his likes and dislikes openly and there was no one to make him feel ashamed and guilty. Although still somewhat reserved, he flourished during his college years. And then came the death of his grandparents, one at a time. His inheritance was sufficient to support him comfortably if not extravagantly for life even if he chose to never seek employment. When his parents died three years later, his wealth tripled. Now he had the luxury of both the time and the money to extract his revenge from the society that had denied him so much.

He felt that his work was absolutely necessary. The world had no right to force their standards and requirements on him. He needed to show the universe that their rules meant absolutely nothing. To let them know that there was no way that they could impose their will on him. He had the power to destroy them as they would soon see. Soon, very soon.

After a hot shower to rinse all the reminders of the day's labor from his body, Brian couldn't resist taking a ride into town to see what the sidewalks looked like when they were crowded with happy and smiling vacationers. He wanted to see what they all looked like so that he could imagine those same faces in a couple of days when they would be wrought with terror.

Brian arrived in Caseville at about the same time that the sun was disappearing into Saginaw Bay. It was still almost eighty degrees. After a lengthy search he found a parking place and set out on foot. He walked up and down in front of all of the colorful lights in the windows of the gift shops and other tourist traps, listening to the reggae music blaring from the speakers that sat on collapsible stands in the doorways. The town definitely had the feeling of Trinidad. Brian felt just a little out of place because he seemed to be one of the only people in town who wasn't wearing a brightly colored tropical shirt covered with images of palm trees and surfers. He ducked into the busy liquor store on Main Street and bought a bottle of his favorite coconut-flavored rum. As busy as the place was, he was surprised to see that they actually still had anything on the shelves. He wound his way down through the side streets where his Durango was parked, jumped in and pointed the nose south, headed for home. He had just barely passed the city limits sign when the car following him suddenly displayed flashing red and blue lights on its roof. Brian was frozen with fear as he pulled over to the shoulder of the road. Something was terribly wrong. He hadn't been speeding so there was no reason for a traffic stop. It had to be something else. The cops were singling him out for something. He ran down the power window and sat with both hands near the top of the steering wheel staring straight ahead. He remembered the Glock in the glove compartment and shuddered. It was a legal gun and he had a permit to carry it but its presence might easily give a cop a reason to look a little farther. Brian was frightened.

"Good evening," said the officer who Brian recognized as Chief Gallagher, "May I see your license, registration, and proof of insurance?"

Brian didn't like the fact that it was the chief. That could mean that he was a specific target. He dug in his wallet and produced the documents that the officer had requested. He handed them to the cop and put his hands back on the steering wheel partly to show respect but mostly to steady his shaking hands.

Chief Gallagher looked in the window and smiled, "Do you know why I pulled you over?

Brian had no idea. "Was I going too fast?"

The cop chuckled. "No sir. It's more than thirty minutes past sundown and you're supposed to have your headlights on. Would you please turn them on now?"

Brian felt a wave of relief pass over him. It was nothing but a routine traffic stop. If this flatfoot wanted to write a ticket, he would gladly accept it. "Oh, wow. I guess that the way the town is all lit up I didn't even realize that the sky was getting dark."

"Not a problem, drive safely," responded Gallagher. He handed all of Brian's paperwork back to him, smiled and said. "Enjoy the festival." He walked back to the police cruiser.

Brian felt very relieved as he drove away but he couldn't help but think of just how fragile and vulnerable his plans were. He quietly resolved to stay within the relatively safe confines of his private sanctuary.

Chief Gallagher found the business card that Michael O'Conner had given him when they first met and he dialed the number.

"O'Conner Investigations. Michael O'Conner speaking. How may I help you?"

"Hello, Mister O'Conner. This is Caseville Police Chief Gallagher. I just made a traffic stop on the subject that you're investigating. I wanted to let you know that he's in the area."

"Thanks. We've been checking out his place. What did you stop him for?"

"Nothing really, just his headlights. He sure seemed jumpy though. I thought he was going to wet his pants." Gallagher laughed.

"I've put together a pretty good group of investigators to keep an eye on things, using some off-duty conservation and peace officers," said Michael, "You were there for our first meeting. Would you like to continue to be included?"

"I've heard that your group has expanded," answered the chief. "I talked to Dee when I brought the patrol boat back to the harbor today. She gave me some interesting possibilities to chew on."

"Okay, I'll make sure that you're in the loop from now on."

Chief Gallagher responded, "If anything happens down on that bathing beach, it's my jurisdiction so I'll need to be up to speed on everything you get."

"I apologize for not including you from the beginning but we really didn't know what we were dealing with. As a matter of fact we still don't have a shred of evidence."

"I understand," said Gallagher. "We wouldn't be

looking at this at all if it wasn't for your investigation. If there turns out to be some substance to it, it's going to mean a hell of a lot if we have a head start."

CHAPTER 41

"I sure hope your phone is fully charged this morning," said McCoy. "We've got a lot of calls to make."

"You know it," said Michael. "How do you want to split them up? Think we should start by making a list of questions so that we can be sure we're both asking for the same information?"

"Okay, let's do it over breakfast." McCoy was already headed for the door.

"Y'know, I'm getting a little nervous," said McCoy as he polished off his western omelette. "It's Monday already and we're into the third day of this here festival. I'm wondering if we shouldn't station a really inconspicuous boat somewhere down near this Brian's place to make sure he doesn't come steaming out of his harbor with a boatload of huge man-eating fish in the next week or so."

Michael stared at him for a moment. "That's not such a bad idea. I might call Bonnie this afternoon and ask her if she'd be willing to pop for something like that. Man, I hate to keep asking her for this stuff. Her bill is already well over five grand and that isn't even including expenses. But then I'd rather have her tell me that it's too expensive than have her ask why the hell I didn't cover that base. We might be able to find one or two old retirees with aluminum runabouts and cell phones that wouldn't mind anchoring out in Wildfowl Bay and keeping their eyes open for a couple hundred bucks a day."

After leaving a message on Bonnie's voicemail about hiring someone to keep an eye out for any boats leaving Brian's dock, Michael and McCoy spent at least five hours talking to aquarium suppliers. They were specifically asking for the buyers of bull sharks who provided their own pick up service. The specific nature of their inquiries helped narrow down their search. By the end of the day they had identified a dozen customers who had purchased one or more bull sharks in the last four months and had provided their own transportation. There were none in Michigan.

Michael kept going back over the records desperately trying to find some common link. There were several outfits who had bought pairs of sharks specifying a male and female. He dismissed them as breeders. A number of them were single purchases and they all needed to be checked out. But what caught Michael's eye were three orders for three sharks each and the orders were about three weeks apart, the destinations were all in Pennsylvania, New Jersey, and Maryland, clustered loosely together.

"Do these three look like they could be related to one another?" asked Michael, "I know that they were sold to customers in three different states but once the delivery truck picked them up there would be no record of where they actually wound up being dropped off."

McCoy was looking at the computer screen over Michael's shoulder. "Hey Mike, can you bring up that picture of that tanker truck in Brian's yard? The one that shows the rear end? I'd like to zoom in on that license plate again."

"Sure but as I recall it's too blurry to read."

"Yeah, I know," said McCoy, "But it wasn't a Michigan plate and I'd just like another look."

Michael opened the picture file and located the photo they were looking for. McCoy squinted for a better look. "I'm a hundred percent sure that it's a Pennsylvania license plate. Can you contact the dealer's who sold the sharks and see what trucking company picked them up?"

"Not a bad idea." Michael wrote a note to himself. "I want to consolidate all of our questions and try to make just one more inquiry so that we don't become pests calling too often. So far we're getting good cooperation and I don't want to screw that up."

Just then Michael's phone rang. It was Bonnie. "Sorry it took so long to get back to you but if you think that watching Brian's place from out in the bay will give you an early warning, I'm all for it. I don't imagine that it will be too expensive. I'd never forgive myself if something happened that could have been prevented by something that simple."

Michael thanked her and signed off.

McCoy was shaking his head. "Y'know, if we tried to put together an operation like this through the police department, we'd still be begging for approval for some of the things that we did four days ago. This investigation wouldn't get moving until about a week from now and the way I figure it, everything would be over by then. Things sure go a lot smoother when there's no red tape and the person in charge wants nothing but results."

McCoy was already dialing Deputy Waldecker's number. "This guy's always got his ear to the ground. I'm betting he can come up with exactly what we need before sundown." He talked with the sheriff's deputy for about five minutes ending the conversation by confirming both his and McCoy's cell phone numbers and hung up with a smile on his face. "He's going to have his dad do it. Says the old man just loves playing James Bond."

It was getting close to five o'clock and the two detectives had bundled what they hoped were the last round of questions to ask the aquarium suppliers. Michael printed out the list and took it over to the motel office and faxed it out to all of the dealers. The letter had included his email address and asked if they would respond electronically. He hoped that he'd have a few answers by morning.

McCoy suggested that they visit the bathing beach again to see if the late afternoon crowds were as large as the mid-day throngs. "Good idea," said Michael and they headed for the parking lot.

As they stood looking out over the sunburned swarm of humanity, McCoy remarked, "I'd say it's off by about thirty percent. Probably because the nightly concerts start in about an hour and a half and they've headed back to feed the kids, clean them up and then wipe them down with mosquito repellent for star-filled evening of calypso music and limbo contests. It's a great life."

Michael grinned. "You're really getting into the carnival mood aren't you?"

"Ya gotta admit, it's mighty contagious."

They climbed back into their car wearing their flowered tropical shirts and cut-off jeans and slowly cruised Main Street in the four block long downtown area. There had to be at least five thousand people crowded elbow-to-elbow, stopping to sample cheeseburgers of all varieties before ducking into a beer tent to find something that would wash it all down. The merchants' cash registers were ringing like casino slot machines and probably bringing in about as many dollars. The classic summer weather was just what the doctor ordered for a successful outdoor festival.

CHAPTER 42

Brian was up early Tuesday morning. There was a lot of work to be done and he'd need to get started right away. As he opened the door to leave his house, he stopped for a few minutes to admire his handiwork on the old fishing trawler. Aside from the shape of the hull itself, the cabin cruiser disguise worked amazingly well. You'd almost have to be an old-time boater to see the mismatch. He was convinced that it would do the job.

He trotted down to the boathouse and dragged his scuba gear out to the dock. Transferring the sharks from their pen to the floating cage was going to be the most challenging part of the job. The cage, with its rear hatch open, was already backed up tight to the gate across the front of the pen. Once he opened the gate on the shark pen, the trick would be to lure the sharks into the cage and keep them up near the front end while he moved the cage far enough away from the pen to give him room to close the rear hatch on the cage. Once that part of the job was done, the sharks would be securely contained in their temporary new home and the rest would be easy.

Before he got started Brian decided to run back to the house and go up to the third floor where he had a commanding view of the bay. He grabbed his powerful binoculars and surveyed the scene. There were a few of the regular sailboats making lazy arcs in the water searching for a breeze but there was no sign of the pesky River Dancer. Aside from an old man anchored in a solitary small aluminum boat with a fishing rod hanging over the gunnel, the bay was quiet. He went back to work.

It took almost an hour to drag the floating island out of the way from where it bobbed over the top of the shark cage. He had to use the barge for that task and it was a clumsy and awkward vessel. After retrieving a half dozen whole hams from the cooler in the back of the boathouse he donned the wetsuit and scuba gear. The rest of the job would be underwater work. He opened the three hatches on top of the cage up near the front end and securely tied the six hams, wrapped in wire mesh nets, to the inside of the cage. Then he swam around the perimeter about ten times double and triple checking all of connections and joints. After securing the top hatches and satisfied that all seams were tight and escape proof, he climbed onto the dock to begin the next phase. It was just about noon.

Brian's hands shook as he turned on the sniffers and exhaust blowers down in the engine room in preparation for starting the twin diesels. When the all clear light came on, he fired up the engines one at a time. The transmissions were in neutral and after a brief warm up, the engines idled smoothly. The cage was still securely attached to the front of the pen holding everything in place. With the sun almost directly overhead he had a good view of the cage floating just a scant 12 inches below the surface of the clear water.

As Brian raised the large door at the front of the boathouse he could see that the sharks were all restlessly clustered at the front gate having sensed the presence of fresh meat. As soon as Brian activated the electric hoist to lift the gate, all nine sharks darted for the hams and began furiously attacking them. Brian quickly released the cables tying the cage to the pen and rushed to the controls of the trawler. He shifted into forward and very slowly moved the entire unit ahead 10 feet. Throwing the transmissions back into neutral he rushed to the stern of the trawler and pulled on the rope that would release the rear gate on the cage and allow it to slam shut. Once closed he had to secure the top latch and attach the quick-opening springs so that, when the time came, releasing the sharks would be instantaneous. When he had finished that part of the chore he anxiously leaned over the transom of the boat with his 'look box' in hand and stuck the snout of the underwater viewing device about six inches below the surface of the water so that he had a clear view of what was going on in the cage. The sharks were still in the midst of a feeding frenzy and were riling up the water so badly that it was impossible to count them. Brian figured that it would be twenty minutes or so before they quieted down enough for the silt and plankton to settle. In the meantime he secured the trawler to the pilings to prevent it from drifting. The last thing he needed was to have his boat run aground in the narrow channel with a cage full of hungry sharks in tow. He looked at his watch. It was nearing 1:30. He shut down the engines and secured all lines to the dock. While he was waiting for the water to clear up, he had kept a close watch on the surface of the channel. No dorsal fins had appeared so he was reasonably certain that none of the sharks had escaped while he was transferring them to the mobile cage. But just to be sure, he needed to take roll call.

Finally around two o'clock the waters were still enough for him to try the look box again. He had a few anxious moments when he could only find eight of his creatures but the ninth one finally emerged from a murky corner, a long strand of pork skin trailing from its mouth.

Brian decided to pull the floating island back in front of the boathouse door. He didn't really need it any more and he'd dismantle it later if he had time. At this point the only real danger of discovery would be an aerial fly over. He'd have to take his chances on that.

Back up in the house, he returned to his perch on the top floor and surveyed the bay. The sail boaters had left and on a normal evening they'd be back for a moonlight jaunt but they were all young folks and with the festival going on in town they would likely spend the night listening to tropical music, drinking tropical cocktails, and wearing tropical flowers in their hair.

The lone fisherman was still out there anchored in the same spot. Apparently the fish must be biting.

For the rest of the afternoon Brian paced back and forth on his dock, racking his brain to be sure he had everything covered. He had checked tomorrow's weather reports repeatedly and they hadn't changed, upper 80s to mid 90s. Sunny and hot with calm winds. A perfect day. Everything was in place and nothing had been overlooked, he was locked and loaded, ready to go. Tomorrow was the day. He continued to pace the dock until the sun disappeared. In the distance he heard a small outboard motor start and accelerate as a boat came on plane. In all likelihood it was the lone fisherman, through for the day. Soon it was just a hum in the distance.

Back in the house Brian made himself another drink, slumped back in his couch and thought about his big event.

CHAPTER 43

Dee worked patrol duty at the county park bathing beach until 7:30 on Tuesday evening and couldn't wait to get away from the enormous crowds that she encountered as she secured the State-owned boat in the Caseville harbor. The fuel tanks had been filled and ready to go on a moment's notice. She jumped into the big pickup truck and headed for the relative tranquility of the Farmer's Bar a few miles east of town. Her cell phone sat in the hands-free device on the dashboard and she used the voice dialing feature to connect to Steve Kraus. "Hey Babe," she hollered into the phone, Wanna meet for a drink at the old place?"

She could hear Steve chuckle on the other end. "You know I'd follow you across the ocean, you sweet thing. I'll meet you there in about twenty minutes."

Dee smiled and signed off. Then she called Michael O'Conner. "Hey Mike, me and Steve are meeting at the Farmer's Bar in a few minutes. You and McCoy are welcome to join us if you want to update us on anything."

"I'll talk to McCoy," said Michael. "He's on the phone with some aquarium suppliers right now but I'm sure he'll want to come along. Plan on us being there."

The Farmer's Bar was really quiet tonight. After all, it was almost the midpoint of the Cheeseburger Festival and things would be absolutely rocking over in Caseville.

Nobody would want to miss a minute of it.

Dee arrived first and was feasting on an order of deep-fried mushrooms when Steve walked in the door. Steve went straight to the bar, grabbed a couple of Bud Lights and pulled up a chair at Dee's table. "So what's up?"

"I was just thinking about the shark theory that McCoy's been trying to sell everybody," said Dee, "The more I think about it the more possible it becomes. As a matter of fact, it's borderline probable as far as I'm concerned. This guy has everything he needs to make it work and he's a certified head case with sociopathic tendencies. We just can't afford to dismiss it. As a matter of fact, I'd say we'd better be prepared to deal with a half dozen or more mature and hungry sharks swimming in Saginaw Bay."

"Okay, I'm in," replied Steve, "What do you need from me?"

"If the fish are swimming free we'll need firepower to take them out. That means rifles, bang sticks, and people trained to use them. We very well could be in close proximity to the bathing beach and can't afford to have projectiles ricocheting off of the water and into the crowd."

Steve nodded. "Two questions. When do you expect this to happen and how do you want me to help?"

Dee swallowed another mushroom and offered the plate to Steve. "Tomorrow is Wednesday and the party ends on Sunday so we've got to be ready from now on. And hell yes, I want you on board for the duration. If it really happens, we'll need all the firepower we can get. This isn't a police operation at this point so I don't need to worry about unauthorized civilians at a crime scene. Waldecker won't give us any static on this and neither will

Chief Gallagher. They both know you and they both know all about you. They're both sensible cops. I'm planning on talking to them tonight after we hear what Michael and McCoy have to say."

As if on cue the two detectives walked in the door, embarrassed grins on their faces and their brightly flowered tropical shirts lighting up the room. Dee giggled at the sight.

"Yeah, yeah, I know," said McCoy, "More damned tourists polluting your pure country air. We're city guys. What you see is what you get." He shook hands with Steve, saluted Dee and sat down. Michael didn't say a word, he just pulled up a chair.

"Anything new in the shark world?" asked Dee.

"I think so," said McCoy, "We've got a total of nine mature bull sharks that were delivered to non-existent locations and they were all transported by the same carrier and that trucking company doesn't show up anywhere on our radar either. It's starting to look pretty serious."

"He's right," chimed in Michael, "Even I'm beginning to have some faith in this wild speculation. There's a tanker truck parked on Brian's property that very well could have been used to move big fish. It sure looks like it's built for that purpose."

"I see," said Dee, "I don't like the sound of all this. We'd better be ready to roll right now. Did you say that you had somebody watching Brian's place from out in the bay?"

"Yes, but it's not twenty-four hour surveillance. I think we'd better change that right away," answered Michael, "Deputy Waldecker set it up for us and we haven't had any reports yet. I'm thinking that I'd better call him." Michael stood up and moved away from the others while he dialed his cell phone.

"Do you guys have any rifles?" asked Dee.

"Not with us," answered McCoy, "But we're both very experienced with long guns and we're both excellent marksmen. Is that what you think it's going to take?"

Dee nodded. "Once they're free it's pretty difficult to round them up and we don't have the equipment for that kind of operation anyway. If they're hunting for food they'll be swimming near the surface and should be easy to spot. Our best option is to shoot them but it won't be easy. A boat isn't exactly a bench rest, you know."

"We can't get rifles and ammo anywhere at this time of night," said McCoy. "We'll have to find a sporting goods store in the morning and then we'll need a trip to a rifle range to get them sighted in. There's no way that we can be ready at the crack of dawn."

"Don't worry about that, I've got some pretty decent rifles at home," said Dee. "They're deadly accurate and all set to go. I'll bring them with me in the morning. I should be there before six."

Michael returned to the table. "Well, Waldecker says that his dad sat out there all day long and from where he was anchored he had sort of a half-assed line of sight on the boat house and a big cabin cruiser that was in the channel. Says there was no sign of the trawler. I thought that was a little weird because the only cabin cruiser that I've seen on that property is in no shape to even float. I gotta wonder where this mystery boat came from and what happened to the fishing trawler. Anyway he says that Brian was out there working nonstop on something all day. At one point he fired up the engines on the big cruiser but it never left the channel. I guess that our man stuck around watching things until just a few minutes ago. He's planning on heading back out there before five o'clock in the morning. He figures that Brian was working hard to get things ready for something and all the activity stopped around five this afternoon. Sounds like he's all set and ready to move. The old man has a cell phone and so I told Waldecker to give him my number so that he can contact me as soon as there's a change in anything. It sounds like it's real close. My money is on tomorrow. It's supposed to be sunny and hot and that means the beach will be extra crowded."

Steve spoke up. "There's a huge parade in town tomorrow. It's the centerpiece of the whole festival. It kicks off at six o'clock in the afternoon so most of the beach goers will be wrapping things up around 4:30. Everybody attends the parade."

"So I figure that the most likely window will be somewhere between noon and two o'clock," said McCoy. "We've got what? Three boats?"

"Four if you count me," said Steve. "But I'll be coming from a few miles south of here."

"What does your boat look like?" asked Michael.

"It sure doesn't look anything like a big old cabin cruiser," laughed Steve. "It's a 24 foot Four Winns Bowrider. It's easy to spot because there's a big tubular framework that stands 6 feet high over the pilot console. When it's headed straight toward you it looks like something from outer space coming to gobble you up. You can't miss it."

"Okay," said Michael. "We've got a plan. Me and Mc-

Coy will be at the dock around five o'clock. The sun should be just about to come up. We'll see you then."

Steve Kraus prepared his boat when he got home. He hauled one of his favorite rifles out of the gun safe and locked it safely away in the moisture-proof box on his boat. It was his pride and joy, a Remington M-24 system 7.62 millimeter sniper rifle fitted with a Leupold M3 ten-power scope. The trigger pull had been honed to an even 2.5 pounds. He had bigger guns in his arsenal like the 50 caliber long-range sniper rifle but something like that would be much too powerful, capable of sending its payload through a concrete wall at a range of well over a half mile. Steve had all the confidence in the world in his Remington. Coupled with his custom hand-loaded cartridges, he could light a match at 1000 yards.

He secretly prayed that the rifle could remain locked safely away in the foam padded fiberglass box. Tomorrow just might turn into an ugly day.

CHAPTER 44

The old Ford Ranger bounced and rattled its way down the gravel roads. It was late on Tuesday afternoon, an hour or two from sunset and Shorty and Sharon Stueber were headed home to their little ordinary-looking mobile home that sat in a long neat line of ordinary-looking mobile homes. Shorty insisted on avoiding the main roads. He still feared the wrath of the maniac who was chasing him. They had run out of options though and had to leave their safe haven. Sharon' brother had become so antagonistic that Sharon had spent the previous night crying. Besides, Shorty knew that it was time for him to man up and face the music. He had seen an innocent man savagely ripped apart by man-eating sharks, a sight that he'd never be able to put out of his mind. He had to do something about it. He had to do the right thing.

On the kitchen table of their mobile home lay the business card of a private investigator. They should be home by around ten o'clock and then he'd suck it up and call this O'Conner guy. He'd tell him everything he knew and then wait for the hammer to fall. Shorty knew that he'd be in trouble but had no idea how serious it would be. If he had to go to jail, he'd go and Sharon would wait for him. He knew she'd wait.

The park manager was standing in the entrance road when they pulled in the driveway. He flagged them down. Shorty was relieved to see that he had a smile on his face.

"Howdy folks," he said, "I suppose you know that there are a couple people trying to get in touch with you."

Shorty leaned across the seat feeling all of the color drain from his face. "Who? What do you mean by a couple?"

"The first guy, I didn't get his name but he seemed like somebody you'd probably want to avoid but the second guy was, let me see now. Oh yeah, his name was O'Conner. Private investigator. Acted like he was willing to help. And it appeared that he knew a few things about the one who was here earlier. Are you in some kind of trouble? Is there anything I can do?"

"We'll let you know, Art," said Shorty. "You did a great job of running that first guy off the other day. I was inside and heard the whole thing. We've got a few things to take care of at the house and then we'll probably talk. I appreciate you looking out for us."

They parked the old pickup on the concrete pad next to their trailer and then went inside. Sharon found Michael O'Conner's business card and handed it to Shorty as he flopped into the chair at the kitchen table.

"Sounds like this detective might already know something about the goings-on at that house on the bay. Didja hear the park manager?" Shorty was turning the card over in his hand without reading it.

Sharon nodded and moved the telephone from the small shelf on the wall to a spot directly in front of Shorty. Now he had the card in his hand and the telephone in front of him. There was nothing left to do except to make the call.

Shorty fumbled with the card. He was feeling lightheaded. He knew that what he was about to do could very well get him charged with murder and he had no means to defend himself if that happened. He had to just do the right thing and pray that the cops would see it that way. He picked up the receiver and began punching in the numbers.

CHAPTER 45

McCoy and Michael were back at their motel room discussing the likelihood of Brian launching an attack on the City of Caseville. Everybody in their group had agreed that all signs pointed to Wednesday being the most likely day. The parade would insure that the biggest crowd of the week would be in town. The blazing sun would drive record numbers to the beach, and their reconnaissance had revealed that Brian had spent the entire day Tuesday getting prepared for something. They were still debating the possibility of sharks being involved. Michael was having a hard time swallowing it. There was such a slim chance of success in an operation of that nature that it just seemed like a fantasy. But who could take the chance?

Michael's cell phone, plugged into the charger over on the desk began chirping. He stepped over and picked it up. The name on his caller I.D. was Sharon Stueber. He answered immediately and was surprised by the sound of a man's voice on the other end. "Hello, this is Wallace Stueber. Am I talking to Detective O'Conner?"

"This is he," answered Michael as he switched the selector to speaker phone so that McCoy could hear both sides of the conversation loud and clear.

"I've got a lot of stuff to tell you and some of it is probably gonna sound completely crazy," began Shorty.

"I'm anxious to hear it," said Michael, "And I don't care how crazy you might think it sounds."

There was a pause and then Shorty began. "First of all I want you to know that I ain't done nothing wrong. I mean I was just in the wrong place at the wrong time and never lifted a finger to hurt nobody. It was all his fault."

"All whose fault?" asked Michael.

"I never knew his last name but his first name is Brian, at least I think it is. He hired me to do some work around his place, fixing up an old fishing boat and some other stuff. Things was going pretty good. He liked my work. Even told me so. Anyways he drives me into town one evening and drops me off at the bar so's I can play some Keno and I run into this guy that I used to work for about three years ago. The guy was being a real jerk, calling me names and just raggin' on me. I tried to ignore him but we had kind of a shouting match anyways. I was glad when Brian showed up to pick me up. I think that the guy who was giving me all the guff must have followed us home. I'm sure that the other people in the bar seen me leave with that Brian guy. Driller wasn't even in the bar when we left."

"Did you say Driller?" asked Michael.

"That ain't his real name," said Shorty, "They just call him that because he puts in wells for people." Shorty hesitated.

"Go on," said McCoy.

"It was the next day," said Shorty, "Brian told me that he had to run into town for something and I stayed behind working on the boat. Well, I had to use the bathroom and seein' as how there's nobody around I decided to just go in the bay. I was standing next to the old boathouse, one of those buildings that's built right over the water so's you can pull your boat right inside. Well, I thought I heard some noise coming from inside. I knew that I wasn't supposed to go in that old boathouse but my curiosity got the best of me. I found an unlocked window and snuck inside. It was pretty dark in there but I could tell that there was something mighty big swimming around in the water. Then I hear someone moving around outside and I think Brian's back. I don't want to get in no trouble so I squeeze in behind some old crates and baskets that are stacked up in the back of the building.

"I'm hiding back there and I see this Driller guy climbing in the window. I figure if I just stay quiet, he'll look around a little bit and then leave. Like I said, it was pretty dark in there so I knew he couldn't see me. Before he could get his eyes used to the dark he stumbled over something and fell in the water." Shorty paused again.

Michael tried to keep his voice as calm as possible. "What happened then?"

Shorty gulped down a tear. "Something attacked Driller. It was like there was a whole bunch of them. I know we don't have no sharks around here but that's sure what they looked like. They was gigantic fish and they kept ripping at him and Driller just kept screaming and screaming..." Shorty's voice trailed off to painful sobs, "I didn't have nothing to do with it. You just gotta believe me. It was a terrible accident and there was nothin' I could do to help him. Nothing at all."

"We believe you," said McCoy.

"I was too scared to even run," said Shorty, "I stayed hid for a long time. Too long because Brian came back.

He came right into the boathouse and turned on one of the lights. He was all mad because he thought it was me who fell in with them big fish. And he knew that they'd kill somebody 'cause it sounded a lot like he was planning to throw me in there some day. Anyways, Brian jumped in his car and went somewhere and that's when I made my break. I've been running ever since." He started crying again.

"Are you at home?" asked Michael.

Shorty regained some composure. "I'm home and I won't run away. I've done all the running that I'm gonna do. I'll be here waiting when the cops come for me."

"There won't be any cops coming to arrest you," said McCoy, "But they'll probably need you to tell them the same story that you just told us and sign a statement saying it's true to the best of your knowledge. Nothing more."

Shorty sighed in relief. "I'll be here."

Michael and McCoy made sure that they passed on Shorty's story to Deputy Waldecker, Chief Gallagher, and Officer Dee Phelps. In a hasty conference call, Dee suggested that their best chance for success would come if they could somehow keep the sharks contained. It sounded as if Brian was planning to make his move sometime tomorrow and in order to be successful, he would need there to be a lot of people at the beach. That meant that it would be unlikely that he would start too early. If they could converge their police boats on Brian's little lagoon at dawn, they might have a chance. In the event that Brian was already underway, the next best chance was the inlet that surrounded the city's bathing beach. It wasn't a pleasant option but they'd have virtually no chance of success if the sharks were released in the open waters of the bay.

Everybody bumped tomorrow's schedule up about an hour.

And then Michael made the most dreaded call. He had to let Bonnie Prescott know what he had discovered.

CHAPTER 46

It was just before three o'clock in the morning when Sam Waldecker slid the old Sea Nymph out of its hoist and started the ancient Evinrude. His son, the sheriff's deputy, had filled him in on all that had transpired in the last eight hours or so. Sam was convinced that he was about to become a critical part of this tactical operation. Sam had never been a cop but years ago he was an Army Ranger and that sort of training has a way of staying with a man. He quietly motored his way into the calm waters of Wildfowl Bay. After shutting down the outboard motor he silently slid the Danforth anchor over the side and felt it catch in the sandy bottom. A fishing pole over the side, slouched against the backrest on the seat, cell phone in his shirt pocket, and an old fisherman's hat pulled low over his eyes completed the image. Sam waited for the sunrise.

Brian carried the large cooler full of ice water down to the dock and hefted it onto the deck of the boat. One more trip back to the house to grab his binoculars and portable police scanner and he'd be ready to cast off the lines and head for open water. The sun would soon be rising over the waters of Lake Huron on the other side of Michigan's thumb-shaped peninsula and before too long it would be peeking over the treetops on its way to a majestic presence in the eastern sky. Brian fired up the twin diesels and let them perk themselves into an easy rhythm as they came up to operating temperature. Satisfied that all systems were operating normally he slipped the mooring lines from the pilings and pointed the trawler out of the channel in a westerly direction. All of the GPS coordinates were superimposed on the navigation chart that lit up the screen of the laptop. The entire unit was nestled in a special cradle that was built into the control console.

He was taking no chances of anybody tracking his movements from his dock to the public bathing beach so he set a course for Point Lookout on the opposite shore of Saginaw Bay just north of the town of Au Gres. He would travel across the bay and from there he planned to circle northward around Big Charity Island and approach Caseville from the northwest. The maneuver also gave him several options for an escape route.

As Brian worked his way through the shallows of Wildfowl Bay he noticed the dim outline of that same old fishing boat with the same old man anchored in the same place he had seen it yesterday, the fishing pole hanging motionless over the side. He wasn't sure what to make of it and it was still too dark to clearly see any details. There had always been a few fishermen in the area from time to time during the course of the summer and sometimes they got started before daylight. But they usually didn't show up on consecutive days. There was no way he could get closer to the fisherman for a better look. The sandbars and shoals in this part of the bay were unpredictable and always shifting. He tried waving to the old man as he passed but got no response. He finally concluded that the old guy was probably asleep. Just the same, he turned on the police scanner and began monitoring radio traffic.

When the man in the cabin cruiser waved, Sam's old Ranger training kicked in and he remained as motionless as a sniper. Through squinted eyes he watched as the big vessel moved out of Wildfowl Bay coming within fifty yards of his position. The man at the helm was staring, studying him. Without turning his head, Sam continued to track the cruiser as it reached the shelf that dropped off into Saginaw Bay. Now the man held a pair of binoculars to his eyes and was still watching the little fishing boat. Finally the diesels began to roar as the throttles opened up and the boat picked up speed. Only then did old Sam take the cell phone from his shirt pocket.

Waldecker was waiting for Michael and McCoy as they arrived at the municipal docks in Caseville. He was dressed in his water search and rescue clothes, an abbreviated wetsuit with a sheriff's badge imprinted on the chest. His suntanned legs told the detectives that he spent a lot of time wearing that outfit.

"Good morning. You guys ready?"

"Not as ready as you are," said McCoy.

Dee Phelps was the next to show up and she was dressed much the same as Waldecker.

Michael spoke up. "It looks like you guys are toying with the idea of jumping in the bay. I suppose that it's none of my business but, considering there may be hungry sharks swimming around out there, don't you think you should reconsider?"

Dee laughed and handed McCoy two rifle cases. "Here, they're both 30.06's. One is a hunting rifle and one's military. Don't get either one of them wet."

Chief Gallagher was the last to join the group and he was wearing a standard police summer uniform. "I sure look out of place," he smiled.

It was still mostly dark although the sky was taking on a decidedly red glow. The group held a brief strategy meeting before deploying. Their objective would be to keep their police boats between the beach and any threats coming in from the bay. Dee would be stationed at the southern boundary with McCoy aboard and Waldecker and Michael would be guarding from the north. Gallagher would go solo and patrol back and forth farther out in the bay to run off all of the jet skis and powerboats. Communication would be handled through cell phones in order to keep Steve in the loop. Steve was not scheduled to deploy from the harbor. They felt he would be more valuable if he could trail the subject, departing Sand Point and moving north. The same direction that Brian would approach from.

If any shooting should become necessary, it was absolutely forbidden to fire in the direction of the shoreline. In addition to her rifle Dee had a bang stick which was basically a twelve gauge shotgun slug stuck on the end of a long pole. You had to be right along side your prey and the target had to be within a couple inches of the surface for a bang stick to be effective. They were tricky to use but deadly. And they also required a lot of training. Dee was the only one qualified. It would be her responsibility if any of the sharks slipped between the boats.

The sun was visible on the horizon now and people would be making their way to the beach in about two hours.

Waldecker's phone rang. He looked at the display. "It's my dad. I'll put it on the speaker."

The group gathered around.

"Well, he's on his way. I'm sure that this is the real thing today. He's wearing a disguise though, dressed up like a cabin cruiser. But the boat moves like a trawler. He's towing something too. Whatever it is, it's partially submerged and leaving a hell of a weird-looking wake. It's creating a pretty good load on the engines too. I could hear them laboring. They weren't overburdened though, them old trawlers were built to drag a half a mile of net behind 'em. His course looked to be due west. My guess is he's looking for deep and deserted water so that not too many people take notice."

"Great job, Dad. We've got it covered." Waldecker hung up.

As they turned to go to their boats, a Corvette roared into the parking lot screeching to a halt a few yards from the group. The door flew open and Bonnie Prescott jumped out from behind the wheel. She was wearing spandex shorts and a tank top with a map of St. Croix on the front and a very determined expression. "I know that you're not going to like this but I'm going with you."

Everybody looked at Michael and Michael turned to Deputy Waldecker. "We'd never have got this far if it wasn't for her." Waldecker nodded. "We've got an extra lifejacket."

Bonnie reached back in the Corvette and snatched a pair of Ray Bans and a ball cap with a Detroit Lions logo on the front. "I'm ready."

The boats idled out of the harbor single file. A few early risers were setting up their lawn chairs and lining up minnow buckets on the fishing pier as the three boats made their way out to the open water. The bay was so calm that it looked like a mirror. The morning sun reflecting off the water was absolutely blinding.

Dee's boat was the first to drop off and go on station. As soon as she had the craft anchored she dialed Steve's number. "Hey big guy, get ready for some action today." Dee laughed at Steve's response and then replied. "Nooo… Not that kind of action." McCoy laughed out loud.

With a slightly red face Dee filled Steve in on the fact that Brian had departed his home base and was headed somewhere out into Saginaw Bay. She told him about the strange wake behind the boat and described it as a rather unusual-looking cabin cruiser.

Steve said that his boat was in the water and ready to go on a moment's notice. His big SL242 was much faster and more maneuverable than any of the others. If there was going to be any pursuit involved, his would be the best vessel by far. His location was about one mile from the end of the point so he'd have a clear view of anything rounding the point and moving north. He set up a little observation post on his boat hoist and kept a close eye on the western horizon. He should be seeing something any minute now. By his calculations Brian had left somewhere between thirty and forty-five minutes ago and it was less than an hour's run in calm water at a relaxed speed. The minutes began adding up. It had been more than a half hour since he had spoken with Dee and he surely should have seen something by now. He called her cell phone. "Hey Dee, nothing's moving here. Are you sure that your information is good?"

Dee answered. "Well our spotter did say that Brian's

course appeared to be due west, possibly to avoid encountering any near shore boats. He might be circling northward a little ways out."

"He'd have to go more than ten miles beyond the end of the point to drop behind the horizon," said Steve. "But that could be his plan. He seems to think of just about everything. Why don't you contact the other boats over there with you and tell them not to get caught just looking south and let him sneak up on them from another direction."

"Good idea," responded Dee.

Chapter 47

Nine-thirty in the morning and it was already 84 degrees. The streets of Caseville were flowing with humanity, even at this early hour. There were lines of people waiting for breakfast before they would begin their day of souvenir shopping and gorging themselves on elephant ears and funnel cakes, not to mention cheeseburgers. A band wearing tropical costumes and billing themselves as 'Rhythm of Trinidad' were setting up their steel drums and artificial palm trees in the small downtown park. Looking down the side street next to the park, the colorful crown of the ferris wheel set up in the high school athletic field was visible above the trees. It had already begun to move.

The walkways were noticeably narrower this morning with the presence of tens of thousands of folding chairs that began appearing as early as four o'clock, lining the entire three-mile parade route. At six o'clock this afternoon they'd be filled with enthusiastic fans.

Every gift shop in town had its doors wide open with Jimmy Buffett blaring from speakers just inside the doors, and all of the streetfront parking lots were jammed with temporary booths selling everything from air-brushed tattoos to giant stuffed gorillas. The carnival atmosphere was alive and well in Caseville on this beautiful summer morning.

Long before all of the revelry began, an emergency meeting had been held at the headquarters of the Caseville Police Department. Chief Gallagher wanted the bathing beach closed today but the representative from the County Parks Commission wouldn't hear it. "Not without a court order, you won't," the man said, "It's your job to keep the swimming area safe. Just do it." After hearing the entire list of concerns from Deputy Sheriff Waldecker, including the part about live full-grown sharks being held in a pen by a lunatic less than ten miles away, the two state policemen in attendance said that they'd make a request for additional officers but lamented that they'd probably be strictly land-based. Chief Gallagher said, "That's okay. If something happens out in the water we're going to need help making sure that all of the swimmers make it safely back to the beach."

By eleven o'clock in the morning the regular lifeguards at the county bathing beach had been replaced by Michigan State Police rescue divers and there were seven more sheriff's deputies scattered among the crowd. All of the officers carried radios but had been advised to use encrypted language in their transmissions. They were very possibly dealing with a highly intelligent adversary and it would be presumptuous to think that he wouldn't be eavesdropping.

It was decided that the Caseville Police Department would be best utilized patrolling the streets of town. An extra seventy five thousand people could present a daunting challenge and Caseville's tiny police force was already spread pretty thin. They could only hope and pray that things went smoothly in town today. It was a safe bet that they wouldn't be responding to complaints of things like public urination this afternoon.

The music on the streets got louder as the day wore on. Pink flamingos seemed to be everywhere. There were straw hats, sombreros, hats with long feathers, pirate hats, and hats shaped like cheeseburgers. This festival had earned its reputation by providing plenty of carefree fun for working families, the key words being "working families." Caseville is less than a one-tank-of-gas trip from Detroit, a morning's ride from Cleveland, and an overnight hop from Chicago. Cheeseburger is a place where blue collar people mingle with celebrities and the inevitable politicians. All signs pointed to this year being one of the best years on record.

CHAPTER 48

Brian checked his watch and it was closing in on 9:30. The trawler was lugging a little more than expected but he constantly monitored the vitals of his engines and the temperatures had remained stable along with the oil pressure. He had shifted everything into neutral a few times so that he could check on the welfare of the sharks. They had become a little restless, partly because of the slight temperature drop in the deeper water and also the sensation of water moving over their bodies at eight knots. Otherwise they seemed fine. The cage was on an 18 foot tether to give the propeller-wash room to dissipate. It wouldn't be wise to drag the sharks through that turbulence. Brian was hoping that he'd be able to shut the engines down when he got to his destination and just drift for about fifteen minutes to give the sharks a chance to calm down. So far he was still slightly ahead of schedule and it looked like time would be on his side. His goal was to release the sharks shortly after twelve noon. There should be lots of people splashing around in the water about then.

His GPS told him that it was time to make a course adjustment. As he brought the nose of the boat around to the proper compass heading, he could see the low profile of Charity Island slightly off to his right and the broad expanse of Lake Huron north of him on his left.

Brian's heartbeat accelerated as the shoreline rose out of the bay directly in front of him. The coast was now in sight. By his calculations he was only about a half hour from his destination. Everything about the boat was still functioning normally.

He was hypnotized by the dark thin line on the horizon, his thoughts running back decades. He was nine years old and going for his very first boat ride, at least the first that he could recall. His sister was there too and she was sitting in the pilot's seat while their grandpa stood to the side just to be sure that little Bonnie didn't get them too far off course. Brian remembered how Bonnie giggled the whole time. Brian could have had a turn at the wheel but he declined saying that he didn't feel well. The screaming was back. It had visited him often lately although he couldn't remember the first time he ever heard them. They were human voices all right and they were inside his head. They never formed any words, they just screamed. And today they were louder than ever. Bonnie kept inviting Brian to join her on the wide captain's seat. She was always like that, so willing to share when someone else was watching. Brian just couldn't think that way although he very often hated himself for it. He never wanted anyone to have even a small piece of his fun. Even on that day, he wished that his grandfather would have left Bonnie back on the dock. He blamed Bonnie for the screaming voices. It was about that time in his life that his parents had been called to the school counselor's office to talk about Brian's problems with social interaction. That visit had led to sessions with a therapist and Brian hated that. He remembered riding home from the psychologist's office in the back seat of the car and hearing his mom and dad use terms like, 'psychotic depression,' and other words he didn't understand. He might not have fully grasped the meaning of the words but the inflection was clear, even to a nine year old.

Young Brian was a hostile and uncooperative patient and never once mentioned the screaming voices that often woke him up from his nightmares. The therapist was left with nothing but body language and mood changes to form his diagnosis. In later years Brian would describe his entire adolescence with one word… Nightmare.

But today, Brian was in charge. He was lumbering across the widest part of Saginaw Bay on his way to deliver terror and carnage to the unsuspecting throngs who were laughing and playing on the beach. Looking back over the transom of his boat he could see the swell of water rising from the underwater cage as it trailed off the stern of the trawler. It was a strange sight as if there was a small tidal wave following his boat. The effect was magnified in the calm morning waters. He smiled as he watched the rollers rise and fall in his wake. It nagged on his mind that he'd forgotten to bring along the 9mm Glock. He really saw no situation where he might need it but he wished he had it just the same. The police scanner had been quiet all morning with just a few calls about traffic stops. As the day wore on his worries of the morning were slowly evaporating. If that fisherman that he spotted just off the shore of his property had been a spy, he would have surely been intercepted by now. The problem of Shorty was still in the back of his mind but there would be time to deal with him later. Hell, he couldn't even be sure if Shorty was still alive. He decided not to worry about it. Today was going to be Brian's day and nothing could stop him.

Another quick course adjustment and his heading would send him to Oak Point about three miles up the coast from Caseville. Once there he would turn slightly to the southwest and follow the shoreline right to the bathing beach. He was getting close now and his palms were sweating.

CHAPTER 49

Deputy Waldecker was elected to be in charge of the operation. After all, he was a water search and rescue expert with a resume to support it. He was scanning all points of the compass with his binoculars while Michael sat near the back of the boat doing his best to cheer Bonnie.

It seemed as if the full weight of the situation had just revealed itself to Bonnie. Even though it was she who first raised the flag, she found things hard to believe. She had been briefed daily and so she was aware of the whole scenario as it unfolded. The things that the detectives were uncovering were sometimes surreal, like a fantasy, a story about some nonexistent comic book action figure. But reality was now. She was sitting in a boat with two men and two high-powered rifles. They were waiting for her twin brother. And she was sobbing.

She called out to the deputy. "Why do you have those rifles there?" she pointed to the long guns.

"They're to take out the sharks if necessary," said Waldecker without taking the binoculars away from his eyes.

"And what about my brother? You don't plan on using anything like that on him, do you?" she cried.

Deputy Waldecker stepped down from the front of the boat and sat next to Bonnie.

"Miss Prescott I'd like you to please understand that my first duty is to protect those people." He waved a hand toward the beach. "I've never fired any kind of firearm at a human being and I hope and pray that I'm never forced to. Human life means a lot to me and I would only use lethal force as an absolute last resort."

Bonnie looked toward the shore. There were hundreds of people enjoying the warm water and more than half of them were young children. "I understand," she said quietly. "All I can do is hope."

"We'll be doing everything we can to wrap this thing up without anybody getting hurt," said Waldecker.

Bonnie managed a weak smile and the deputy returned to monitoring the surrounding waters. "Seems like there's dozens of white cabin cruisers all over the bay," he said. "The walleyes must be biting." He put his binoculars down and picked up his cell phone. "I'm going to call Steve in. He's too far away to be of any help if we needed him right now and if anything was going to happen over his way, it would have happened by now."

When Steve answered the call, they held a short strategy session and decided that Steve could zip around the end of the point and run a couple miles to the south to check out Brian's place just to make sure that he hadn't returned home. With Steve's fast-moving boat it would only add about twenty minutes or so to the trip.

Waldecker made another call, this one to Dee to fill her in on the plan. "Not a bad idea," said Dee. "Where do you want to station him when he gets here? Too bad he doesn't have any police markings on that boat. Chief Gallagher could probably use a hand out there. He's running back and forth like a madman shooing boats away from the bathing beach and it's not even noon yet."

"With his speed, I'm thinking that we'll want him back here in the interior. Just in case," said Waldecker.

"Roger, wilco. Are you seeing anything over your way? There must be a million cabin cruisers down here. But we're set up fairly close to the harbor entrance so I guess I understand it. "

"It's the same over here," said Waldecker, "With gas prices the way they are these days, it makes you wonder where the money comes from."

"Credit cards," answered Dee.

In front of his house four and a half miles to the south Steve fired up the 350 cubic inch Mercruiser engine and powered it up to full throttle. He roared west along the shore of Sand Point and rounded the tip in a graceful arc. Sand Point is only about a mile wide but it juts out from the mainland over five miles separating Saginaw Bay on the north from Wildfowl Bay to the south. He set his course for Brian's hideaway about three miles south and cut a diagonal course to his dock. He was there in twelve minutes. Satisfied that there was nothing there except for the old barge tied up at the dock, Steve swung the big boat around and cut a trail back around the point and then up the shoreline to Caseville. The entire operation consumed a little over a half hour. The Caseville harbor would soon be in sight and the bathing beach less than two miles beyond the harbor.

CHAPTER 50

The twin diesels churned at a leisurely pace, power and purpose in their throaty rumble. Brian was making his way slowly along the coast only about three quarters of a mile offshore and a scant mile and a half from his objective. The weather was doing everything that the forecasters had promised. The temperature was climbing toward the ninety-degree mark on its way to record levels. The bay was dotted with pleasure boats and personal watercraft. It seemed as if anything that would float was sharing the near-shore water with him. He had taken one last look at his precious cargo just before he made his last course correction and he was happy to see that the sharks were still quite lively. He could feel his pulse racing as he rounded the last curve in the landscape. Over his left shoulder there were people visible all along the private beaches in front of the endless line of summer cottages. It wouldn't be long now.

Waldecker briefly focused his field glasses on the cruiser approaching from the northeast. It was still too far away to identify but it was coming at them from an unusual direction for a boat of that size. It could be arriving from Port Austin, eighteen miles up the coast he thought. Lots of the tourists heading for the festival preferred the beach side approach, it solved the parking problem for sure. He'd check it again in a few minutes.

His phone rang. It was Steve. "Hello Steve. You headed our way yet?"

"I'm back on the north side of the point and coming straight at you. Shouldn't be more than twenty-five minutes, half hour at most."

"Good," replied Waldecker, "You'll probably see Dee's craft as soon as you're within sight of the bathing beach. You can hook up with her."

"Oh, I'll find her all right," answered Steve. "All of you guys are hard to miss with all of that overhead framework full of blue strobe lights. I'll check back with you as soon as I connect."

Waldecker put the cell phone back in the holder on the control console and returned to sweeping the horizon with his binoculars. Soon his attention was drawn to the cruiser approaching from his right. "Michael," he said. "Come up here a minute and bring your glasses."

Michael scrambled up onto the raised bow of the patrol boat. "What's up?"

Waldecker pointed to the boat coming directly toward them from the northeast. "Check that out."

Michael adjusted the binoculars until he had a fairly clear view. "Seems like kind of a big boat to be running that close to shore. Pushing a pretty good bow wake too, like a dog with a bone in its teeth."

"That's what I thought," said Waldecker, "The front end is riding unusually high too. Why don't you get on the phone and let everybody else know that we've got a suspicious vessel approaching."

Michael returned to his seat next to Bonnie and made calls to Dee, Chief Gallagher, and Steve telling them all what he had observed. Then he turned to Bonnie and put his hand on her arm. “We’ll get through this,” he said, “We’ll *all* get through it.”

Steve knew that he was too far away. Even running at full throttle he was still more than fifteen minutes from arrival, closer to twenty and it sounded like Brian would be there in under ten. He opened the storage box, pulling out his range-finding binoculars and pressed them to his eyes. Caseville was not yet in view.

The two guys in a 35 foot Fountain Lightning were giving Chief Gallagher a rough time. “Hey man, we’ve been doing this all week. We don’t go inside the swimming buoys, we anchor just outside the line and the girls paddle out to meet us on their tubes. We won’t bother anybody. We got a date, man.”

“It’s restricted today,” said the Chief, “No boats of any kind allowed until further notice,”

The guy in the passenger seat spoke up. “You ever seen a boat like this? If we want to, we can blow right past you and be in and out before you even get that little thing in gear.”

Gallagher grabbed his police radio and called the harbor master. In a voice loud enough for the two men to hear, he said. “Have somebody sit on all the trailers in your parking lot. When a blue-and-white offshore boat comes in, MC zero one two four, take them into custody.”

“Any more questions?” he asked

The man behind the steering wheel spit in the cop’s direction and turned the bow of his big boat toward open water and jammed the throttle full forward, his sudden wake almost capsizing the chief’s little boat. Chief Gallagher’s cell phone began ringing and he steadied himself with one hand while he answered. The voice on the other end said. "We're moving to intercept our target entering the area from about twenty-two degrees northeast."

Gallagher, dangerously out of position due to his encounter with the offshore boat, started his engine and set a course to seal off the route to the west. He could see Dee's boat making its way from its station on the south end of the bathing beach. If everything went according to design, they would have the subject surrounded in less than five minutes.

Brian heard the call on the police scanner. It was on the harbor master's frequency. Apparently there was some kind of law enforcement activity out on the water. That was something that he hadn't given too much thought to. Hopefully whatever happened was away from the bathing beach area. He sure didn't need any problems like cops. From his angle of approach it didn't look like much was going on. There were only a few boats in sight and they all seemed to be moving in different directions. Something struck him about the small number of boats milling in the waters off the bathing beach. He wrote it off to the fact that there were larger numbers of people on the streets of town. They probably wanted to be where the action was.

CHAPTER 51

Brian's eyes were focused on the beach. He was close enough that he could hear the kids yelling and laughing. There had to be over three hundred people in the water. He watched his depth sounder carefully. He had set a minimum of 18 feet of water under the keel. He wouldn't venture into anything shallower. He was almost there. He turned the bow away from the shore, gave the cage time to swing around behind him with its hatch facing the beach then threw the transmission into neutral and let the big boat drift to a stop. He was so captivated by the crowd on shore and other distractions like the activity in the cage that he didn't notice the two boats closing in from either side between his boat and the beach.

Leaning over the transom of his boat, Brian could tell that at least most of the sharks had been attracted to the commotion near shore and were trying to bump their way out of the cage. Running back to his controls he jerked on the line to open the hatch. There was a swirl in the water as the first of the sharks bolted from the cage. Now he needed to drop the cage to the bottom and prepare to escape. There was a rush of air through the vent lines and air bubbles rose to the surface as he activated the mechanism that pulled the bungs from the floatation barrels. He yanked on the rope to release the tow line but it stopped short as if fouled. He pulled again and again but the tow line wouldn't release. The cage was now sinking at an awkward angle. Racing back and forth on the boat he checked every pulley and cleat but couldn't find the problem. The release catch simply wouldn't open and now the cage was dragging on the bottom of the bay. The tow line was made of steel cable so he couldn't even cut it. He cursed his planning for not covering every eventuality.

It was only then that he realized that there were two boats moving in ahead of the dorsal fins and that both boats had men with rifles standing on the bow.

Brian started the engines and tried to make a break for open water but the cage had snagged on an underwater boulder and refused to budge. Suddenly the boulder lost its grip causing the boat to lurch forward only to seize the next big rock and bring the boat to an instant stop raising its stern and forcing the bow underwater. The unexpected jolt sent Brian tumbling across the deck. He heard the words, "Clear the bathing area immediately," shouting over his police scanner. The confusion was too much for Brian. Dazed, he sat on the deck, the voices screaming in his head. After all his careful planning, nothing was making any sense.

One shark broke away from the pack and headed straight for shore. Dee grabbed her bang stick and pointed at the big fish, hollering to McCoy, "Get alongside that one." McCoy swung the boat around to an angle that would intercept the path of the shark and accelerated to keep pace with the fast-moving fish. Dee had the bang stick in both hands raised high in the air as they pulled along side. With a force that belied her undersize frame, Dee slammed the business end of the bang stick into the shark forward of the dorsal fin about one third of the way back from its nose. The explosion was deafening and the bang stick recoiled so violently that it almost flew out of Dee's small hands. She managed to hang on and rocked back on her heels barely maintaining her balance. There was no doubt that it had been a lethal blow to the shark as the big fish rolled over, its white underside glistening in the sunlight.

Dee didn't dwell on the dead shark, she quickly looked around and spotted a second shark heading their way and started to yell. McCoy was already prepared for the moment and had the powerful M-1 Garand up tight against his shoulder. He made quick work of shark number two with one round of the premium hunting ammunition. Although the rifle he fired was used to the lighter, less powerful military ammunition, the action was well up to the task and had automatically chambered another cartridge in anticipation of the next shot. It wouldn't be necessary though. McCoy had scored a perfect hit. "Any idea how many there are?" hollered McCoy.

Dee looked out in the direction of the foundering cruiser. "I can see at least four more," she answered. "The other boat is in a good position to take them out. Oh, and it looks like two more coming this way right now. There might be one on the other side of that cruiser too. I thought I caught a glimpse of a fin over there." She pointed to where Brian was now kneeling on the deck of the cruiser which looked to be settling ever so slightly at the stern.

Michael had taken the controls of the sheriff's patrol boat and had Bonnie by his side. She clung to his arm, tears streaming down her face. She could see her brother and the bewildered look on his face as he tried to understand what was going on around him. Brian didn't appear to see Chief Gallagher, still in the distance approaching him from the bay side in the fast-moving police boat and he had not yet noticed Bonnie although she sat staring at him from less than a hundred yards away. Bonnie couldn't stop crying. She was living her own personal nightmare.

Michael was maneuvering the boat into a position between the shore and the cruiser so that Waldecker could have a clear shot at the four sharks that seemed to be circling to get their bearings. The first one was easy. It broke away from the others and swam directly toward the sheriff's boat, most likely being attracted by the commotion that the boat made in the water. Waldecker steadied himself against the tubular steel tower that sat slightly ahead of amidships and squeezed off a carefully aimed shot. It was an instant kill. There was no time to celebrate his expert marksmanship though. The three remaining sharks were beginning to move in scattered directions. He concentrated on the most distant one swimming almost directly away from them and he missed on his first shot. Gathering himself once more, he saw blood splatter the second time he fired. He couldn't be sure where he hit the shark but from the size of the red plume that erupted from his target, he was pretty sure that it wouldn't be a threat any more.

Michael yelled to Waldecker to hold on so that he could swing the boat in toward shore in order to keep their targets on the bay side of the boat. It was a turbulent but necessary maneuver that had them all hanging on. When the boat came to rest they found themselves in a position with another shark headed directly for their broadside and closing fast. Waldecker barely had time to aim but got lucky with another deadly shot. They all looked around but were unable to locate the fourth shark.

Dee was busy reloading her bang stick. "I sure hope I don't have to use this thing again," she said. "They're damned near uncontrollable. Sometimes I wish I'd never qualified with it."

"You sound like you've used it before," commented McCoy.

"Only on alligators," answered Dee as she stowed the weapon in the clips on the gunwale of the boat. "Got a bead on the next one?"

"He's on his way," said McCoy as he shouldered the Garand. He took plenty of time to be sure that the boat had stopped rocking and sent another shark to its grave with a single shot. "Two for two," he proclaimed.

"Doesn't look like we're going to be so lucky with the other one," said Dee. She pointed to the route that the last shark was following and it clearly put Waldecker, Michael, and Bonnie in the line of fire. She grimaced, rolled her eyes and retrieved her bang stick once more. With a quick glance at McCoy she stepped up onto the bow platform and then turned to him. "You know the drill."

McCoy once again brought the boat to a course that would run parallel to the big shark that was following its nose toward the shore and all of the bathers who were finally scrambling for safety.

Dee stood rock still, poised to strike as they moved close to the shark. She had just raised her weapon for the kill stroke when the shark suddenly veered to the right bumping hard into the boat and spilling Dee into the water directly over the back of the shark. There was no time for McCoy to reach the rifle. He immediately killed the power and snatched his forty caliber service automatic from his hip holster. He hurried to the front of the boat and sent seven hollow point slugs directly into the shark's head. The fish continued to thrash as the surrounding water changed from blue to red and with its big eye staring directly into McCoy's, the shark rolled onto its side and surrendered its life.

Dee, treading water a few yards away simply nodded and swam toward the boat. "I wonder how the other guys are doing?" she said as she clambered back aboard.

"There he goes," shouted Michael as the dorsal fin broke the surface of the water. The shark was headed directly away from them following the coastline northward. The fish had a pretty good head start and so Michael had to lean on the throttle to catch up. Fortunately the sheriff's boat was pushed by a 150 horsepower motor and was capable of some respectable speed. They overtook the shark in under ten minutes and lined up for the shot. It was a textbook harvest as Waldecker calmly dispatched the shark with a single bullet. He pulled the police radio from the slot on the control console. "Have we got 'em all?" he asked hopefully.

Dee answered first. "Maybe but I don't really think so. How many did you take out?"

"By my count it was four," answered Waldecker.

"Same number here," said Dee. "But I'm almost sure that there were nine. That means that there's maybe still one out there somewhere. If there is, I'm betting it's on the other side of that cruiser over there."

Chief Gallagher joined the conversation. "I'm in

position to scan for your last renegade. I'll keep my eyes open. In the meantime somebody had better get over this way and get this guy off of the cruiser. It's going down."

CHAPTER 52

Brian's boat was definitely in distress. The shock that the hull took when its tow became fouled with something at the bottom of the bay had apparently opened a seam in the transom. It was listing badly and sitting very low in the water. It couldn't possibly float for another fifteen minutes. Brian was moving around on the deck now obviously disoriented and out of touch with his surroundings. He looked up and recognized the Caseville Police Department boat, its blue strobe light blinking, moving in from the west. When he turned toward the shore he could make out another boat headed his way and this one had a State of Michigan seal on the side. And from yet another direction came a boat with the familiar County Sheriff's logo on the side and one of the passengers on that boat bore an uncanny resemblance to his sister. Too many things happening at once. Too many people closing in on him. Too many voices screaming in his head. He kicked off his shoes and dove over the side.

"He's in the water," reported Chief Gallagher. "I'll try to fish him out." The police boat was closing in but was still separated from Brian by over a thousand yards of open water. Brian, obviously unaware of his surroundings was swimming almost directly toward the police chief.

Deputy Waldecker grabbed his radio and told the police chief that he would move his craft into position to cover the backside of Brian's track. But there was still the strong possibility that at least one shark was unaccounted for… it could be more. He asked Dee and McCoy to hold their station near the bathing beach and watch for any signs of danger in the water.

Chief Gallagher's voice crackled over the radio. "How many sharks have you killed so far?"

"We're pretty sure it's eight but Dee Phelps thinks that she may have seen one swimming in a westward direction and that would have him somewhere out near you."

"Just what I need," said Gallagher. "A swimmer in the water, a man-eating shark searching for his lunch, and I'm all alone in this boat. Hurry up and get here."

Bonnie broke her silence. "If you can get alongside the police boat, I can jump aboard and give the chief a hand so that he doesn't need to do it all himself. I can at least drive the boat or something."

Waldecker paused a moment and then radioed Chief Gallagher with the plan. Everybody agreed that it would be best to maximize their resources and so the sheriff's boat changed course and mad a beeline for the other boat.

As Bonnie was climbing aboard the police boat they heard someone yelling in the water. Brian, about 100 feet away from the two boats had finally realized that he was swimming directly toward them and had panicked. In his haste to change directions he had overextended his efforts and exhaustion had taken hold. He was foundering badly, disappearing underwater twice for more than a minute at a time.

Chief Gallagher dropped his duty belt, the big forty caliber automatic making a loud clunking sound as it hit the floor of the boat, sat down and pulled off his shoes and dove over the side, swimming frantically in Brian's direction. When he reached the flailing madman, Brian tried to fight him off but all of his thrashing had left him too weak to be effective. Gallagher easily got behind him, looped an arm over his head and began dragging him back toward safety.

Steve Kraus was finally getting closer although he was still almost a mile away. Through his powerful binoculars he could see two boats with the blue strobes coming together and somebody from one of the boats climbing into the other. Adjusting the glasses just in time to see somebody dive from one of the boats, he tracked the swimmer and saw him making his way to what looked like someone in distress. The range finder in his binoculars told him that he was still almost twelve hundred yards out, a little over five-eighths of a mile.

In short order things settled down. The rescue seemed to be going well because he could now see that one of the swimmers was pulling the other back toward the boats. The sinking cruiser caught his eye and he switched his focus. He could see the boat's disguise beginning to peel away, the superstructure that Brian had taken from that old cruiser and attached to the deck of the trawler had broken its fasteners and was starting to float free of the fishing tug's hull. Still looking through the binoculars he fished his cell phone out of his pocket. Glancing down only momentarily he hit the button next to Waldecker's name and heard it ring on the other end. As soon as the deputy answered Steve asked, "Hey. What's happening over there?"

"It looks like the chief's got everything under control. He's bringing the suspect in as we speak."

Steve continued to scan the surface of the water as he talked on his cell phone.

Without warning a dorsal fin broke the surface about 40 feet behind the two swimmers and was headed in their direction, gaining steadily.

Steve shouted into the phone, "Everybody. Everybody hold your positions. Don't move no matter what happens. Just don't move."

He shut off his phone and the boat engine at the same time, grabbed his sniper rifle and sandbag rest then ran through the center walkway and threw himself onto the cushions in the forward section of the boat. He set up his sandbag bench rest straddling the bow cleat and laid the rifle barrel in its cushioned notch. His range finder said one thousand forty yards, still a pretty good distance. Not much detail was visible to the naked eye but when he brought the powerful scope to bear he could clearly make out the shark closing fast on the unsuspecting pair making their way back to the police boat.

Steve knew immediately that he was the only one with a chance for a shot. Both the deputy's and the police chief's boats were in a position where they'd be firing directly toward the bathing beach and the sinking trawler sat in between Dee's boat and the target. From Steve's angle, the next landfall was Manitoulin Island, Ontario, over a hundred and fifty miles straight north. It was all open water in between. He laid in the bow of his boat with the riflescope following the shark and waited for the boat to stop rocking in the slight wake that had caught up to him after suddenly shutting the engine down. "C'mon, settle down. Steady. Steady," he murmured.

The shark was on them now and Steve still wasn't able to get off a shot. The shark had grabbed Brian by the right leg just below the knee and was shaking its head furiously trying to tear the limb loose. Finally Steve's boat stabilized and the shark paused, still hanging on. He inhaled then exhaled slowly and held his breath. He slowly put pressure on the trigger.

Bonnie was screaming, running from the bow to the stern of the police boat. Her brother was in the grasp of a hungry shark and the only thing that the police chief could do was keep trying to pull him free. It looked futile. She could see the water around them turning red from the blood. All she could do was scream, "Brian, oh Brian."

The shark suddenly rocketed straight up out of the water, its entire head exploding. It was moments later when the crack of the rifle reached them. They all looked in the direction of the sound and saw a boat in the distance, a small puff of smoke drifting off its bow. Steve's shot had precisely found its mark. Waldecker's phone was ringing. He answered and heard Steve's voice. "Go get 'em," he said.

CHAPTER 53

"There's been a lot of tissue loss and there's only so much we can do as far as reconstruction." The doctor was speaking with Bonnie Prescott. "He should be able to walk again but it will take a lot of therapy and a lot of time. We'll be keeping him sedated for a day or two. The only reason that he didn't lose his leg was that you had a number of people around him with a lot of first aid experience and who understood trauma. It didn't hurt that they had emergency communication capability either."

"I know," replied Bonnie, "The helicopter was waiting when we got to the hospital and they had him down here in Ann Arbor so fast there was still water dripping from his hair."

Brian had technically been placed under arrest as soon as he had been rescued. The collar belonged to the Caseville City Police so there was an officer, a copy of the Miranda warning in his hand sitting with Bonnie in the waiting room. She turned to him. "That was a very brave thing that your chief did out there. When that shark attacked, he could have let go of my brother and saved himself but he didn't. He fought to keep Brian alive. I hope he'll be recognized for that.

"I'm sure he'll get some kind of medal," said the officer, "The city loves giving them out. I've even got a couple and I've never done anything heroic."

The news that reached the public had a slightly skewed spin. The television stations were broadcasting a story about a vessel that accidentally ran aground while transporting some non-native aquatic species to their intended new home in an aquarium near Bay City, Michigan. Some of the fish had become trapped in their collapsed cages and had to be destroyed at the scene. Authorities stressed that while the incident occurred in clear view of a public bathing beach, no one was in any danger at any time.

Shortly after the bizarre news broke on the local television networks Michael's phone rang. It was Shorty. "If I seen what I think I just seen I guess I'm not so crazy after all," he said. "Is there anything else I can do?"

"I'm pretty much out of the decision-making part of it at this point," said Michael. "It's a law enforcement issue from now on. We worked with the cops all through this thing so they're keeping McCoy and me in the conversation. If you want, I can bring you in as an associate of mine and help you get through all the red tape. You've already come forward and it was your tip that set the operation in motion so I'm sure that you won't be implicated. It will be viewed as a cooperative gesture. I'll have to ask you not to talk about this with anybody else though. And don't worry, I'll vouch for you."

"I'm gonna see this thing through. You got no idea what it's like to see a man die and not be able to do nothing to save him. I should've called the cops right away. Instead I ran. I'm done running."

Michael thanked Shorty and told him that he'd be in touch as soon as he knew anything.

Chief Gallagher told the entire group that he wanted them in his office for a debriefing at 9:00 the following morning. He insisted on complete silence regarding the incident until they had a chance to talk.

It was another gorgeous morning when they all arrived. The sidewalks were once again crowded with revelers seemingly oblivious to the high drama that had unfolded less than twenty-four hours ago. The endless rows of cheeseburger grills were fired up and waiting for the first round of hungry tourists.

Bonnie Prescott had left her hotel near University Hospital in Ann Arbor shortly after 5:00 this morning. She insisted on being there. Her Corvette was the first vehicle parked outside the community building today.

Chief Gallagher's appearance was impeccable this morning. He had a relieved smile on his face. In spite of highly dangerous circumstances that didn't seem to be covered in any police training manual, they had come through it with no fatalities and the only injury was sustained by the perpetrator and he would recover.

The chief had enough presence of mind to secure the scene, sending the injured Brian off with Waldecker, Bonnie, and Michael while directing Dee, McCoy, and Steve to recover all of the dead sharks and tow their carcasses to a secure, state-owned cove where they could be brought ashore and transported to the Department of Natural Resources laboratory for postmortem examinations. They needed to know if there were any human remains in any of the sharks stomachs or digestive systems.

It was all Chief Gallagher could do to keep curiosity

seekers away while the rest of the team took care of their grisly task.

In an expanded sheriff's department investigation, the skeletal remains of two or possibly three humans had been recovered from the shark pen in Brian's boathouse. Everything had been turned over to the State Police crime lab for processing.

Now Chief Gallagher had the entire group assembled in his office. "As a police chief," he began, "I cannot condone involving civilians in police activities. It's clearly against all policies and regulations. But this was far from a typical situation. We had no proof that we would be dealing with an unlawful act and were moving purely out of concern for the community. Call it a citizen's preemptive action. Secondly I'd like to humbly thank all of the civilians whose skills, keen eyes, and courage made this operation so amazingly successful."

About The Author

Dennis Collins literally grew up on the beach where this story takes place. His grandparents owned a home on the shore of Saginaw Bay and he spent his first eighteen summers enjoying the sugar sand beach and swimming daily in the cool waters of the Great Lakes. After a career in Manufacturing Engineering he returned to the area and currently lives only about a hundred yards from the house that holds so many of his childhood memories. These days he splits his time between the beach and his Harley. On rainy days he writes mystery novels.